CLUEDLE

5 MINUTE MYSTERY PUZZLES

Agent in Training

Also available:

Cluedle: The Case of the Dumpleton Diamond

Cluedle: The Case of the Golden Pomegranate

Cluedle: The Case of Rudolph's Revenge

Cluedle: The Case of the Silver Cipher

Cluedle: The Case of the Grindstone Goblet

ROCKET FOX

50 FIENDISHLY FUN FAST PUZZLES

CLUEDLE

5 MINUTE MYSTERY PUZZLES

Agent in Training

HARTIGAN BROWNE

First published 2026 by Rocket Fox, an imprint of Pan Macmillan
The Smithson, 6 Briset Street, London EC1M 5NR
EU representative: Macmillan Publishers Ireland Ltd, 1st Floor,
The Liffey Trust Centre, 117–126 Sheriff Street Upper, Dublin 1 D01 YC43
Associated companies throughout the world

ISBN 978-1-0350-8956-7

1 3 5 7 9 8 6 4 2

A CIP catalogue record for this book is available from the British Library.

Printed and bound in the UK using 100% Renewable Electricity by CPI Group (UK) Ltd

FSC www.fsc.org
MIX
Paper | Supporting responsible forestry
FSC® C116313

Visit **www.panmacmillan.com** to read more about all our books and to buy them.

AGENT SELECTION

Greetings! Hartigan Browne here, the world's greatest detective (though I say so myself).

A rare opportunity has arisen at my agency . . . it seems we have too many mysteries and not enough super sleuths to solve them. I am therefore looking for a new recruit to join the ranks, and have received information to suggest that YOU might well be the perfect candidate!

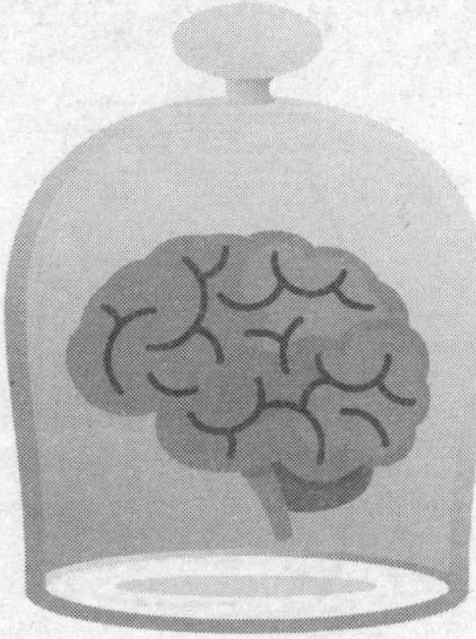

So, young detective, let's see, shall we? Fifty teasing tasks follow that will test your grey matter like never before. What's more, each mini mystery is designed to be cracked in five minutes or under. If you think you have what it takes to join the Hartigan Browne Detective Agency (HBDA for short), then please do turn the page.

Go well!

Task 1: In a Pickle

A little appetizer to begin! My collection of pickles is my pride and joy. To deter my staff from snaffling from the office fridge, I keep the contents of the jars under wraps. Unscramble the letters on the label of each pickled product.

Splendid! Now, can you deduce my preferred pickle?

It:

- contains a double letter.
- does not start with a vowel.
- is fewer than eight letters long.

Write your answer here: ______________________

But why on Earth do I need to know about pickles? I hear you ask.

In my years as a diligent detective, I've learned never to go out in the field without taking a substantial sandwich, packed with pickles. It's the perfect pick-me-up – try one for yourself!

Answer on page 104

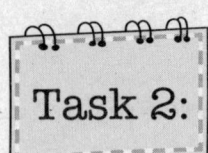

Task 2: Number Crunching

On to more serious matters. Let's see how you are at cracking secret codes, an important skill for an agent-in-training. This time we're looking for a number code.

First, fill in the following grid correctly. Each row, column and 3x3 mini grid must contain the numbers 1–9 only once. The numbers in the shaded squares will give you a 4-digit code when read from top to bottom.

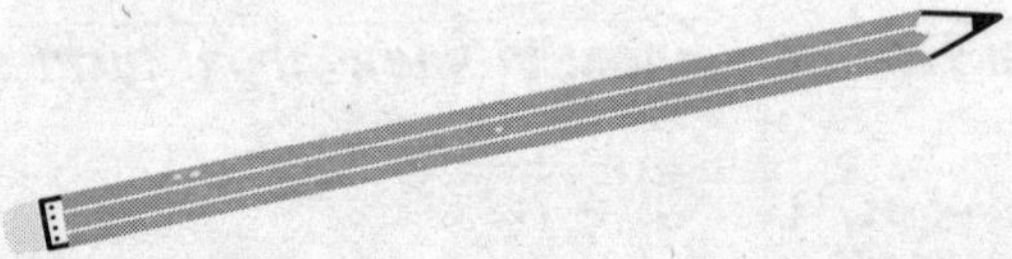

3			9	5		4	1	
9	4		1	8		5		
6	1			2		8		3
7	6		5	4	8			9
	3	4		1		2	5	6
5	9	1	6				8	
2			8		1		4	
1	5	6	3	7	4			8
4			2	9	5	6		

Now punch in the code:

Answer on page 104

Task 3: Ride the Bus

All of my agents must possess an excellent sense of direction, whether travelling over land, sea or through outer space. I confess we *are* still awaiting a case that requires rocket travel, though it never hurts to be prepared.

Can you work out which London bus will take you to the correct destination? Clue: It is the only bus that displays a prime number.

Workings out:

Write your
route number
on the bus:

Excellent! You are heading in the right direction. Continue your journey making sure to keep your eyes peeled for any hint of danger.

HARTIGAN'S HINT: Remember, a prime number is only divisible by itself and 1. For example, 7 is a prime number.

Answer on page 104

Task 4: On the Fence

Any candidate wishing to join the HBDA must familiarize themselves with all kinds of different ciphers. Suspected jewel thief Ruby Rouge is on the move . . . I need your help to track her down. We can't be too careful, so I'm passing on my instructions in code.

Are you familiar with the Fence Cipher? So-called because it looks like a picket fence. Try to transcribe my message.

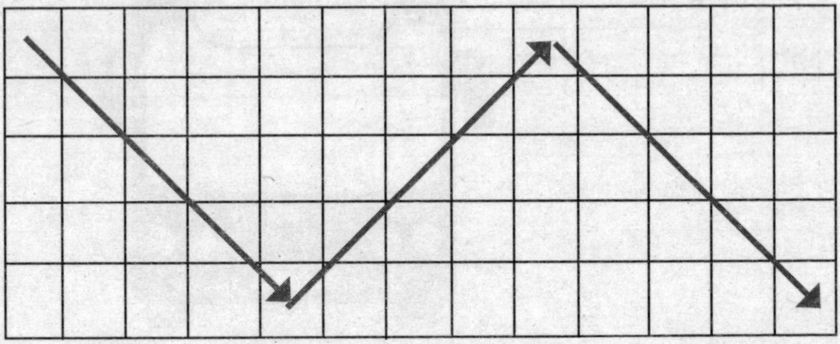

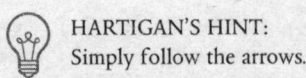

HARTIGAN'S HINT:
Simply follow the arrows.

F	L	O	W	B	I	T	T	E	R	B	Y	E
B	O	X	E	D	A	T	R	I	D	I	N	G
C	E	L	L	B	L	A	C	K	A	C	R	E
H	O	W	L	T	W	I	N	C	H	T	A	P
A	C	H	O	O	S	O	C	K	S	T	A	R

Answer here: _

T	H	I	N	K	B	L	O	C	A	Y	P	O
H	A	R	B	O	U	R	A	N	K	L	E	S
E	L	K	B	O	W	L	B	R	A	C	E	D
H	O	P	E	D	B	E	R	R	Y	B	A	G
C	H	A	D	A	D	E	S	D	O	B	I	B

Answer here: _

I do hope you weren't stumped by the Fence Cipher! Now make your leave post-haste . . . we've a thief to catch.

Answer on page 105

Task 5: Spare Key

I'm sending you to an address believed to be the hangout of a villainous crew of pickpockets. Before you try to enter, you stay in the shadows until you're sure that no one is at home.

You arrive to find the main doors padlocked with thick chains. There's no way of breaking in without heavy-duty cutting equipment, so you scoot down the steps to the cellar door.

There, on the floor, is a crate of rusty-looking keys. At first glance, the keys seem to match into pairs, until you discover that only one does not have a duplicate – let's hope it's the key you need!

Sort the keys into pairs, then fill in your answer in the box opposite.

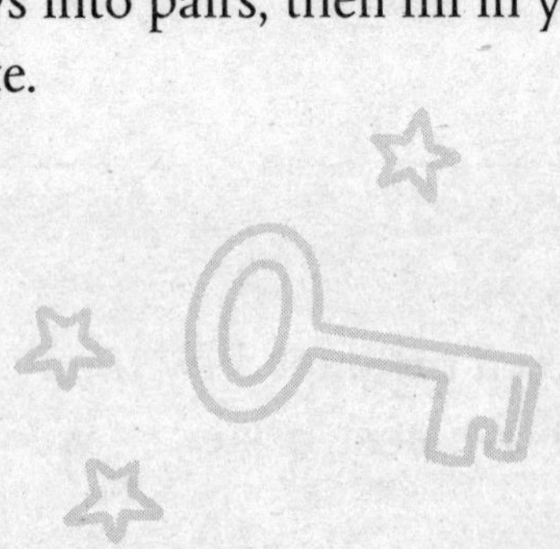

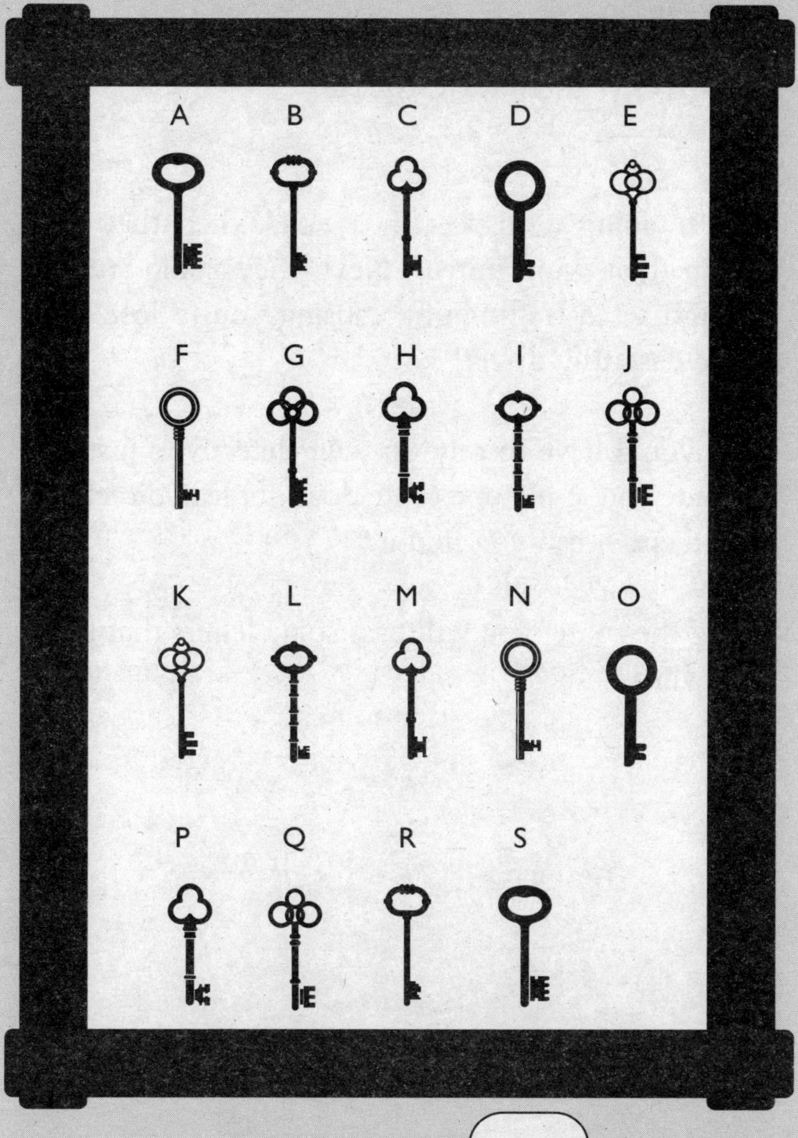

Which key is the odd one out?

Answer on page 105

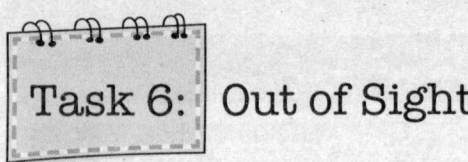

Task 6: Out of Sight

You're tailing a suspect in a taxi, when they spot you in their wing mirror. Next, they zoom straight through a red traffic light, causing you to lose sight of the dastardly driver!

Now you'll have to rely on your detective's instincts to guide you. Only one route does not lead directly to a dead end – can you find it?

Along the route, you will pass some letters that make up a word.

HARTIGAN'S HINT:
The correct destination contains more than one vowel.

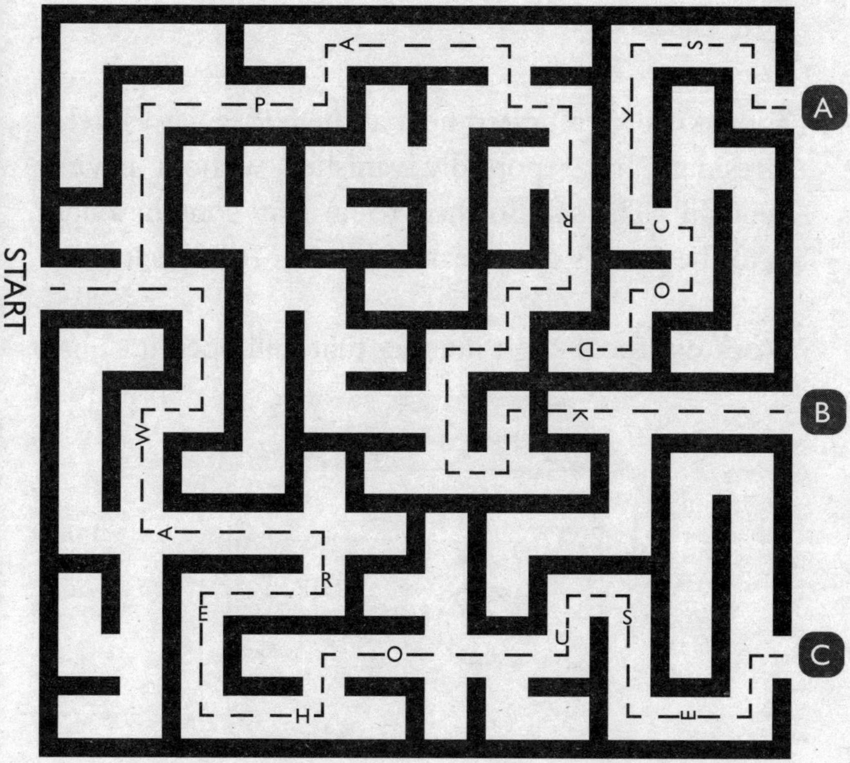

Write the driver's destination here:

___ ___ ___ ___ ___ ___ ___ ___ ___

Answer on page 105

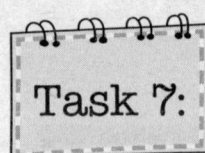

Task 7: Play it Safe

Your skills are required next at the Hideaway Hotel – a resident has reportedly vanished without paying their bill. The safe in their room may contain a clue as to the guest's disappearance, but it remains locked.

Work out the 4-digit number that will open it.

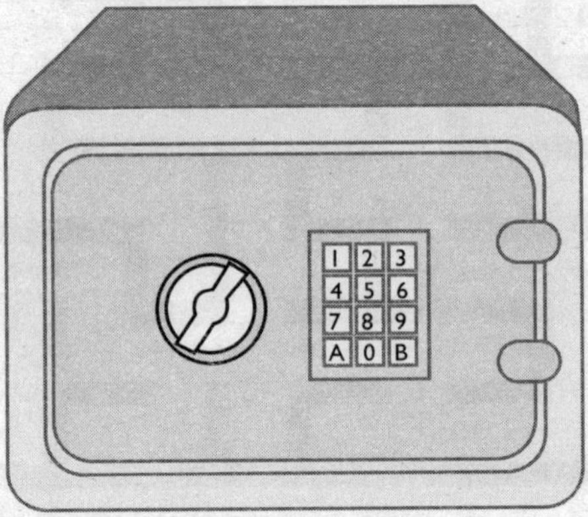

This is a number pyramid. To find a missing number add the two blocks below it. E.g. 2 + 3 = 5

HARTIGAN'S HINT:
To work out a number below a block, use subtraction.

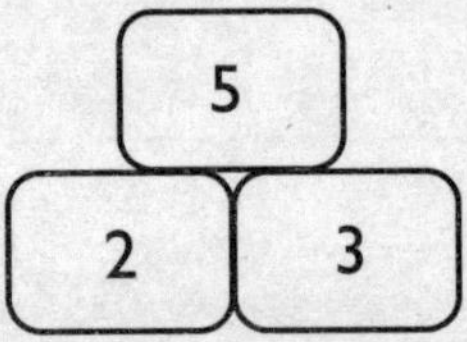

The code to the safe is the only 4-digit number, found at the very top of the pyramid.

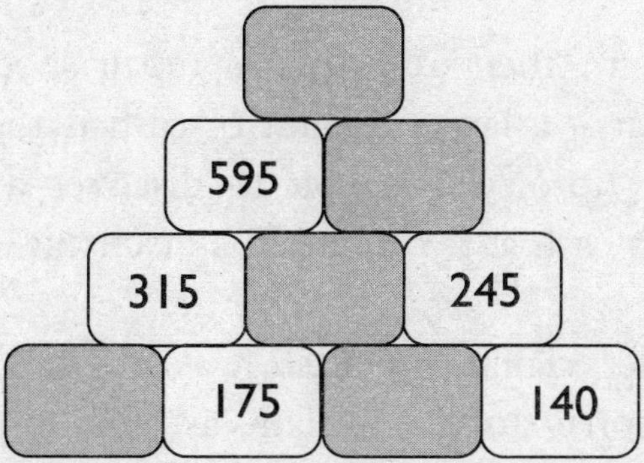

Workings out:

What's the code?:

Answer on page 105

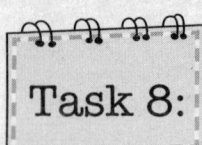

Task 8: Money Laundering

There's been a theft from the car repair shop Wheel Fix Any Car – a large amount of cash is reportedly missing. A tip-off leads you to discover a holdall stuffed with cash at the home of a mechanic.

Axel Muffler claims the cash was a gift from his granny, a sorry story, especially as most of the £50 notes inside the bag are covered in engine oil!

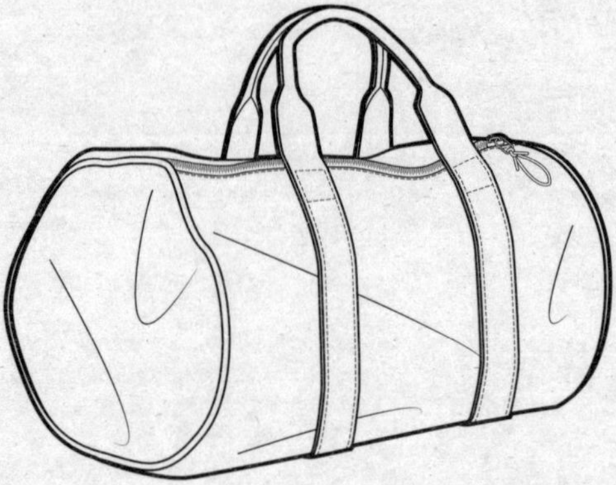

Count and collect the money. It will be important evidence.

Workings out:

How much money is in the bag? **£**

Answer on page 106

Task 9: Dine and Dash

A crime has been reported at the prize-winning restaurant Dolci Divini. After scoffing two portions of the most expensive dish on the menu, pasta with white truffle, two diners scarpered without paying their bill!

It appears the crime was thirsty work – the perpetrators have left their fingerprints on a glass bottle.

You put on a pair of disposable gloves and dust for prints. There may be a match on the HBDA database of suspicious characters back at HQ.

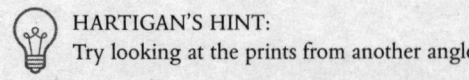

HARTIGAN'S HINT:
Try looking at the prints from another angle.

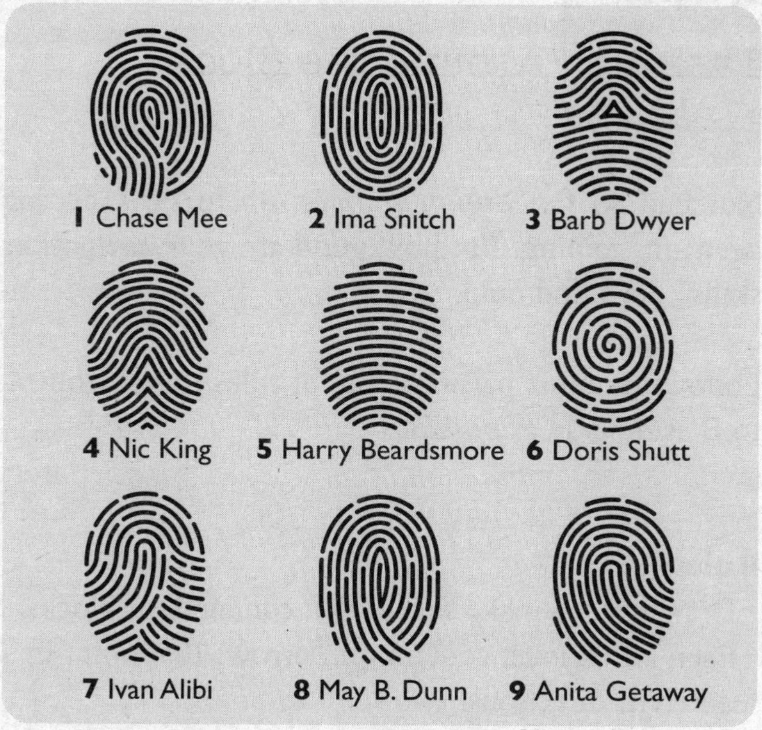

Fingerprint **A** matches with number: ______

Fingerprint **B** matches with number: ______

The dine-and-dash duo were:

____________________ & ____________________

Answer on page 106

Task 10: Around the Block

Not bad so far! You're shaping up to be a decent agent-in-training. But how good are your navigation skills? Let's find out.

Follow my most particular set of rules to get from A to B as quickly as possible.

Rules:

- Draw lines to make shapes that contain four blocks.
- Each block must contain four arrows that point in different directions.
- No arrows should be left over.
- The shapes may be rotated or flipped.
- No shape should have more than six sides.
- The first shape has been added for you.

HARTIGAN'S HINT:
A trusty pencil and eraser will allow you to easily correct any mistakes.

These are the shapes you need:

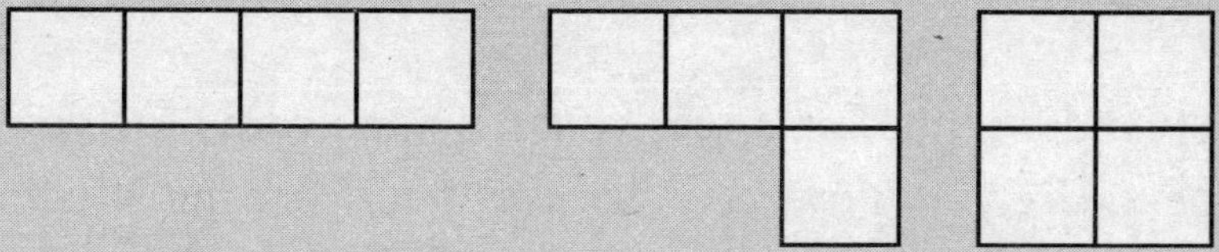

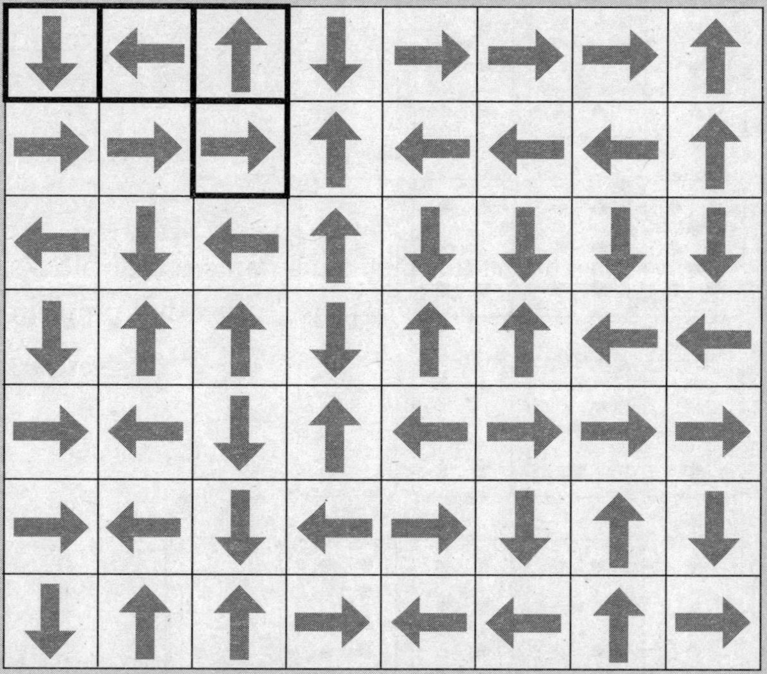

Answer on page 106

Task 11: Card Trick

Splendid stuff! Let's see what's on the cards for you next. Use your powers of deduction to work out which playing card comes next in each of these sequences.

A

B

C

D

E

HARTIGAN'S HINT: You'll need to be in your prime to figure out sequence E.

Easy, no? Well, there's more to this puzzle than meets the eye.

The answers reveal the time a crime was committed, the name of a suspect and what they stole. Can you deduce the details?

Time: ____ . ____ ____

Name: ________________________

Item stolen: ________________________

HARTIGAN'S HINT: The answers from A–C will give you a time, D the name of the suspect and E the item that was stolen.

Answer on page 107

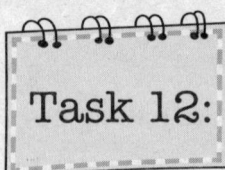

Task 12: Malicious Message

You are awaiting instructions to solve your next detective dilemma when a message flashes up on your phone screen. Curiously, it's from an unknown number, and it's been encoded using the Caesar Cipher.

The message isn't from me, I'm afraid – a crafty crook by criminal means has somehow got your number!

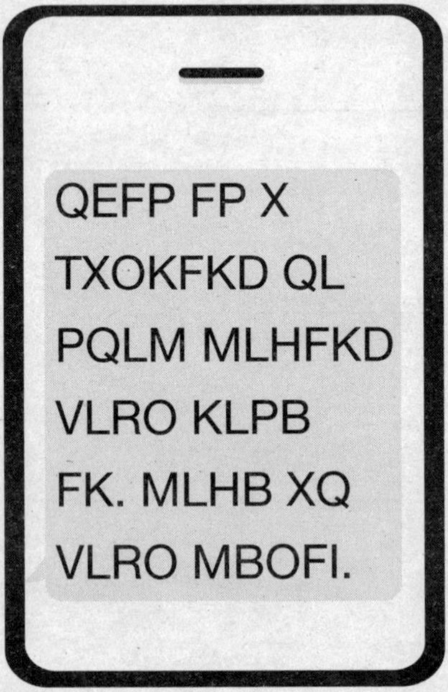
QEFP FP X
TXOKFKD QL
PQLM MLHFKD
VLRO KLPB
FK. MLHB XQ
VLRO MBOFI.

This cipher is named after Julius Caesar, who used it in his private correspondence. I have started to work out the code but it's up to you to complete the rest of the cipher wheel. Make sure to count the same number shift each time.

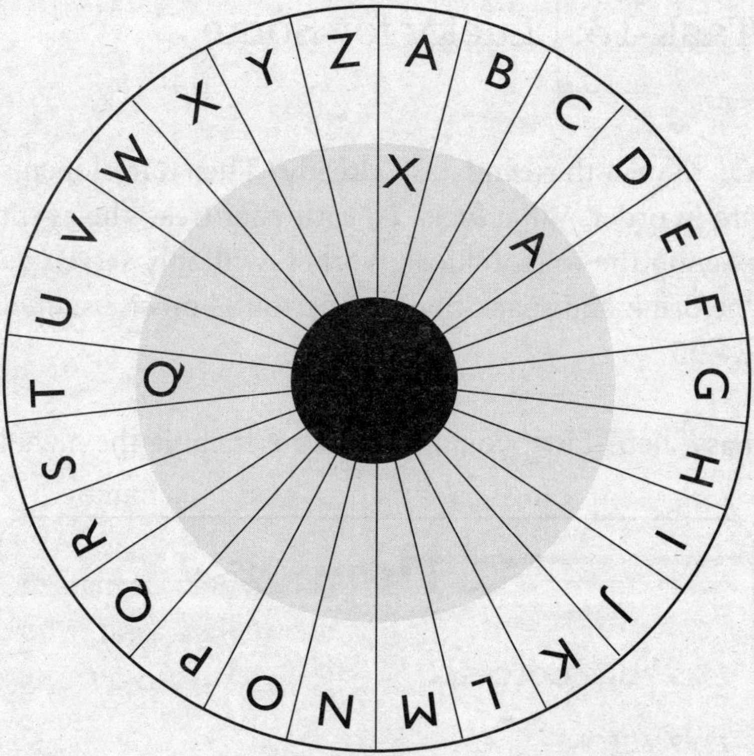

Write your answer here:

_ _ _ _   _ _   _   _ _ _ _ _ _ _

_ _   _ _ _ _   _ _ _ _ _ _

_ _ _ _   _ _ _ _   _ _ .   _ _ _ _

_ _   _ _ _ _   _ _ _ _ _ .

Answer on page 107

Task 13: Lucky for Some

On to your thirteenth task already? Then refreshments are in order. What luck! To earn your treat, the agent playing the role of 'kiosk worker' will only serve you the drink and snack that add up to the precise sum of £4.95.

Easy, heh? First, you'll have to unscramble the menu!

Menu

£3.25	TOH COOLCHEAT	_ _ _ _ _ _ _ _ _ _ _ _ _
£3.49	ECFOFE	_ _ _ _ _ _
£2.50	EAT	_ _ _
£3.00	GRANOE CEJUI	_ _ _ _ _ _ _ _ _ _ _
£1.75	TREWA	_ _ _ _ _
£2.75	JAPFALCK	_ _ _ _ _ _ _ _
£2.25	EKCA	_ _ _ _
£1.95	ECOKOI	_ _ _ _ _ _

Now work out which drink and snack add up to £4.95.

Write the correct drink here:

____

Write the correct snack here:

____

Lemon squeezy! You are duly handed your refreshments. Nice work, detective!

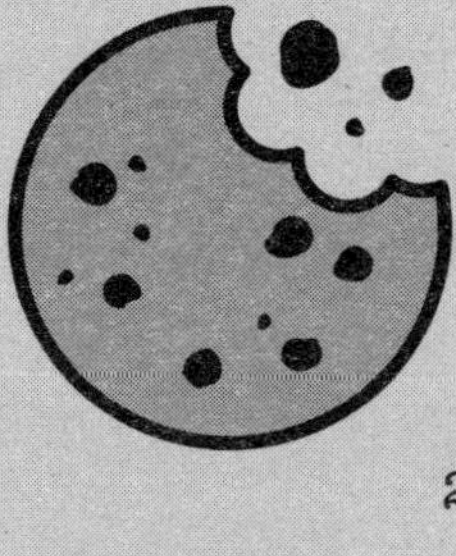

Answer on page 108

Task 14: In the Frame

There are many ups and downs in the life of a detective, much like this next code – the Zigzag Cipher!

I've received the nod from another of my agents that a priceless painting is the target of a theft planned for tonight. Encrypted in the message below is the name of the artwork.

If you're not familiar with this cipher, fret not! All you need to do is to read from left to right, following the letters in the zigzag pattern.

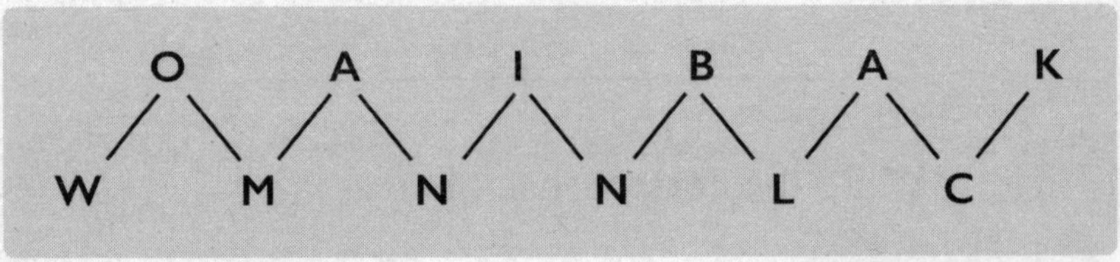

Answer: ___ ___ ___ ___ ___

___ ___ ___ ___ ___ ___ ___ ___

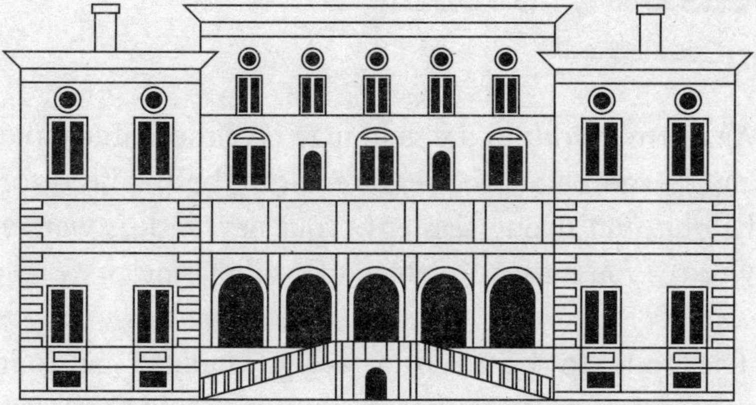

My agent has also shared the name of the museum, soon to be the scene of the crime. Can you work it out?

```
  U   E   M   F   I   E   N   F   N   Y   R
 / \ / \ / \ / \ / \ / \ / \ / \ / \ / \ / \
M   S   U   O   F   N   A   D   A   C   A   T
```

Answer: __ __ __ __ __ __   __ __   __ __ __ __

__ __ __   __ __ __ __ __   __ __ __

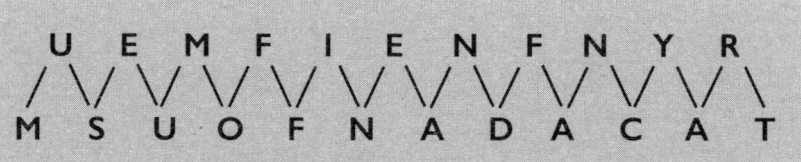

Excellent work! We best make haste . . . there's priceless artwork to save.

Answer on page 108

Task 15: Subbing In

An agent's work in the field may take them above the clouds and below the seas, requiring both a head for heights and strong sea legs. Your next task is watery work – you must gain entry to a submarine!

The code to board is a 4-digit number of four consecutive numbers that touch. It may read forwards, backwards, up, down, but not diagonally.

For example:

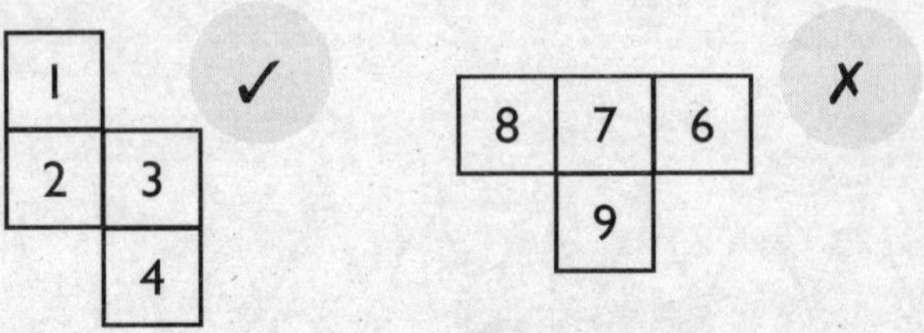

Find the 4-digit code in the grid below.

6	4	7	1	6	6	4	9
4	7	5	6	2	3	7	0
1	8	9	3	4	1	8	4
0	6	4	9	7	0	5	3
6	3	6	4	2	3	4	6
4	6	8	1	9	3	6	5
7	5	2	3	5	4	9	7
0	6	1	8	6	4	8	9

Now punch in the code: ☐ ☐ ☐ ☐

Phew, you're in! No sub-standard performances here.

Answer on page 109

Task 16: Data Breach

Only yesterday I extracted some data from the laptop of a local crime boss. However, when I logged on today to share the details with you, the file was corrupted! Blasted technology! Instead you'll need to study the clues and use logic to work out which suspect lives where.

Clues:

1. Wendy's house number is half that of Mad Dog Doug's
2. Baani doesn't live at No.11 but she does have a blue door
3. One suspect lives at No.22 Mole Avenue
4. No.11 has a black door, but it's not on Tinker Hill

Read the clues, placing ticks and crosses in the grid as you collect the evidence.

		Suspect			Road Name			House Number		
		Mad Dog Doug	Wendy the Weasel	Baani Bander	Tinker Hill	Catcher Crescent	Mole Avenue	11	22	33
Door Colour	green									
	black									
	blue									
House Number	33									
	22									
	11									
Road Name	Mole Ave.									
	Catcher Cres.									
	Tinker Hill									

Bravo! We better hurry and interview our suspects.

Answer on page 109

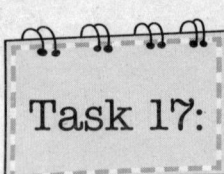

Task 17: Planetary Problems

The agency has just received a worrisome phone call from a Dr Cressida Hawking at the planetarium. Some important elements of their solar system display have been pilfered!

Now's the moment to show your star quality! Complete the cosmic word search using the words below. Words can go up, down, across or diagonally.

Four Letters

Mars

Five Letters

Earth

Venus

Six Letters

Uranus

Saturn

Seven Letters

Mercury

Jupiter

Neptune

				T	Y	P				
			Q	R	E	R	N			
		U	R	A	N	U	S	P		
	I	L	M	E	R	C	U	R	Y	
M	H	S	I	Y	E	B	M	D	A	G
G	A	N	E	P	T	U	N	E	C	O
E	A	R	T	H	I	D	G	K	S	I
	Z	U	S	K	P	M	Z	U	K	
		S	A	T	U	R	N	D		
			B	D	J	E	Y			
				E	V	C				

Now rearrange the letters in the shaded squares to work out exactly what has been stolen.

1. _____ _____ _____

2. _____ _____ _____ _____ _____

HARTIGAN'S HINT: Try starting with words that share a letter.

Answer on page 110

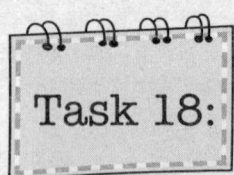

Task 18: Sneaker Scam

You're tailing a suspect thought to be involved in the smuggling of counterfeit goods – designer sports shoes, to be precise. The shoes on his feet are kind of a giveaway!

But when the suspect suddenly picks up the pace, you struggle to keep up. Luckily, a crumpled ball of paper falls out of his pocket in his rush to get away.

You open out the paper to reveal a series of strange symbols. It appears to be a message encrypted using a cipher known as the Pigpen Cipher.

Here's how to decode the curious cipher, in case you've not come across it before.

Key:

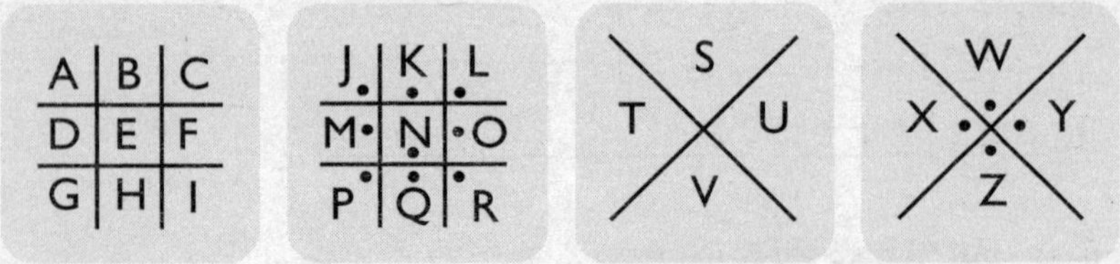

Decipher the message as quickly as you can and write your answer below the symbols.

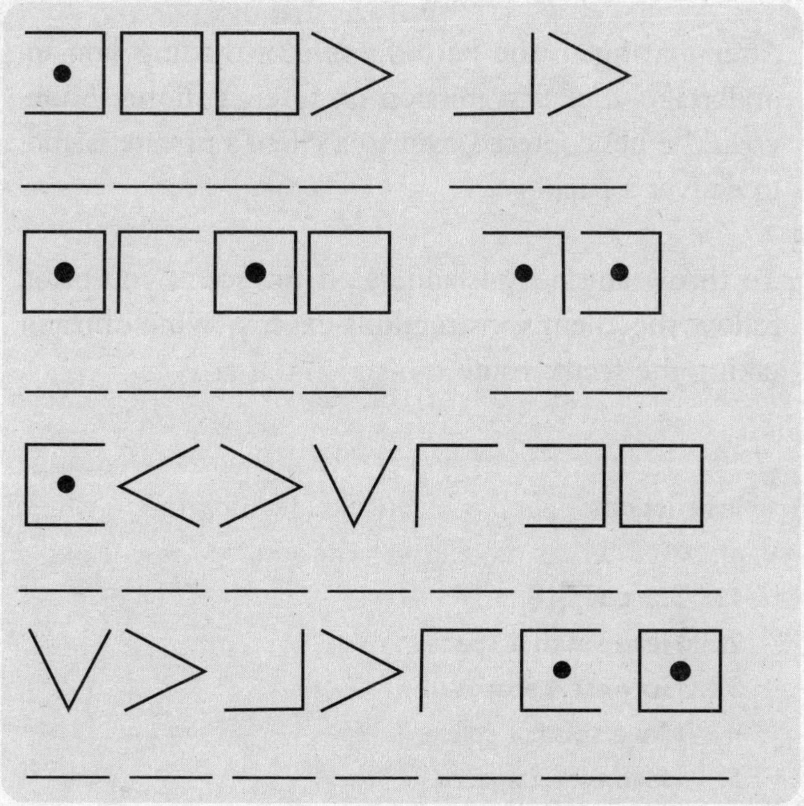

Bravo! You're a super sleuth! You pass on the info to the police, and later learn that the crook was safely taken into custody.

HARTIGAN'S HINT: Each shape represents a letter on one of the four grids, e.g. A = _|

Answer on page 110

TOP SECRET

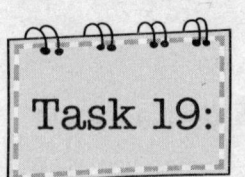

Task 19: Island Tour

After putting in the hard yards, I'm trusting you to undertake your first mission on foreign shores. Soon you'll be helicoptered over to a client's private island to deliver a package.

To throw any nosy islanders off the scent, you must follow the client's instructions exactly, which means taking the scenic route.

Instructions:

1. Start at G, 6.
2. Head south 1 space.
3. Go west 4 spaces.
4. Move south 1 space.
5. Head east 2 spaces.
6. Travel south-east 1 space.
7. Go east 2 spaces.

What are the coordinates of your delivery location? Write the letter first, then the number.

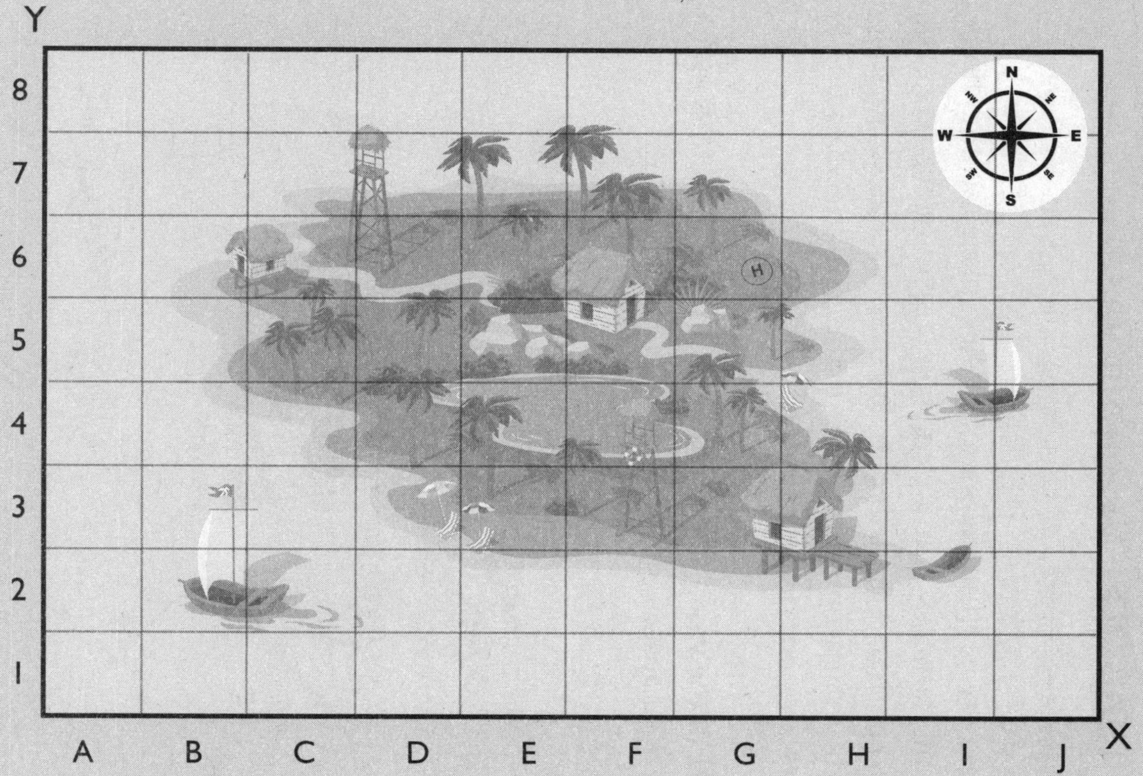

Answer on page 110

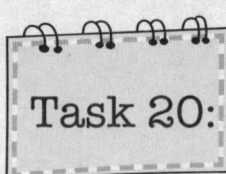

Task 20: Valuable Vase

Your next investigation takes place at the home of Baroness von Reich, where a burglary has been reported. You arrive to discover it's less of a break-in than a breakage – the baroness's prized vase is in pieces on the parlour floor.

Put the vase back together by adding the letters in the right spaces.

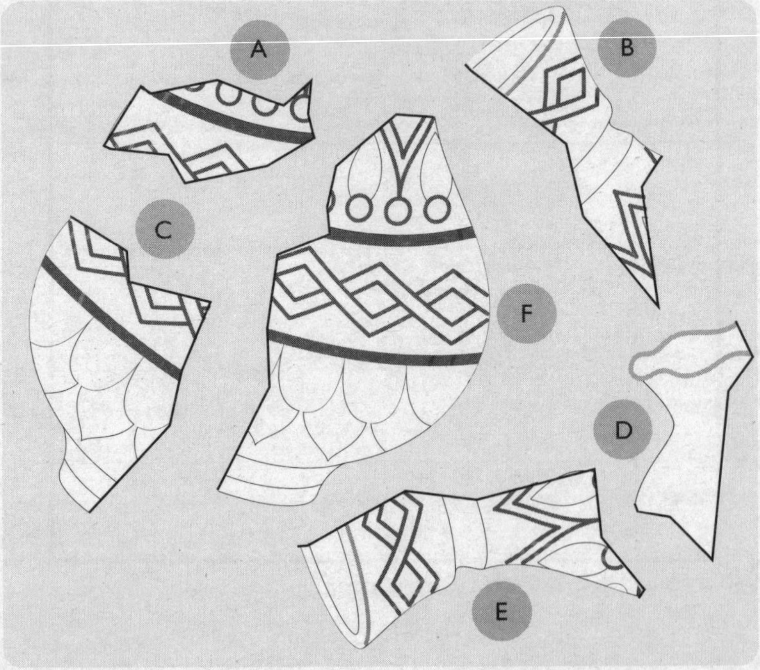

You pick up the pieces to discover there's one extra . . . the broken vase is a counterfeit! From the baroness's red face it seems likely the break-in was staged! Let's not waste any more time here.

Write the letter of the extra piece:

Answer on page 111

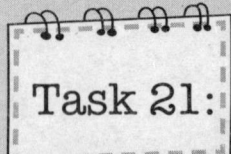

Task 21: Alpha Bravo Charlie

As an undercover underling, knowledge of the NATO phonetic alphabet is a must. It was invented by the military as a way of spelling things out on the telephone or over the radio so that each letter is understood correctly and quickly.

No more 'Did you say 'F or S', 'M or N'? Not only does this amazing alphabet save time, it might just save your life! When spelling out each letter, a code word is used.

Work out the four dead drops in my list:

A = ALPHA	J = JULIET	S = SIERRA
B = BRAVO	K = KILO	T = TANGO
C = CHARLIE	L = LIMA	U = UNIFORM
D = DELTA	M = MIKE	V = VICTOR
E = ECHO	N = NOVEMBER	W = WHISKEY
F = FOXTROT	O = OSCAR	X = X-RAY
G = GOLF	P = PAPA	Y = YANKEE
H = HOTEL	Q = QUEBEC	Z = ZULU
I = INDIA	R = ROMEO	

1. HOTEL–OSCAR–TANGO–ECHO–LIMA

___ ___ ___ ___ ___

LIMA–INDIA–FOXTROT–TANGO

___ ___ ___ ___

2. PAPA–ALPHA–ROMEO–KILO

___ ___ ___ ___

BRAVO–ECHO–NOVEMBER–CHARLIE–HOTEL

___ ___ ___ ___ ___

3. BRAVO–UNIFORM–SIERRA

___ ___ ___

SIERRA–TANGO–OSCAR–PAPA

___ ___ ___ ___

4. UNIFORM–NOVEMBER–DELTA–ECHO–ROMEO

___ ___ ___ ___ ___

TANGO–HOTEL–ECHO

___ ___ ___

BRAVO–ROMEO–INDIA–DELTA–GOLF–ECHO

___ ___ ___ ___ ___ ___

Answer on page 111

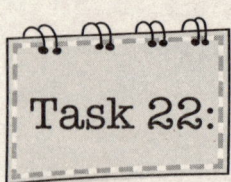

Task 22: Seeing Double

By the hairs of my beard, it appears I have a *doppelgänger*! Someone out there is daring to impersonate me, no doubt with dubious intentions. Study these surveillance photos, then circle the true Hartigan Browne.

A

B

C

D

E

F

Correct, of course! No one forgets Hartigan in a hurry!

Now the imposter has dared to make contact! Can you work out how the message has been encoded and fill in the missing letters?

M _ _ T   M _

_ N D _ R   T H _

V _ _ D _ C T   _ T

M _ D N _ G H T.

C _ M _   _ L _ N _

_ N D   T _ L L

N _   _ N _.

HARTIGAN'S HINT: Think about the type of letters that are missing.

Answers on page 111

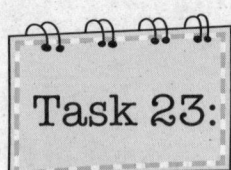

Task 23: Destination: Unknown

You have a suspect under surveillance at London King's Cross Station. Their destination is yet to be confirmed. To work out which train to board, solve this next teaser using the helpful clues:

- The train is not yet boarding.
- The train has not been cancelled.
- The train is due to depart before half-past two in the afternoon.
- The platform contains an even number.
- The platform contains a letter.

WELCOME TO KING'S CROSS STATION

DEPARTURES

Time	Destination	Platform	Expected
13.18	YORK	02A	BOARDING
13.20	NEWCASTLE	11	BOARDING
13.25	EDINBURGH	04	13.33
13.39	INVERNESS	13	ON TIME
13.45	PETERBOROUGH	07B	13.46
13.48	ABERDEEN	06	13.55
14.00	DURHAM	12	CANCELLED
14.05	CAMBRIDGE	08A	14.28
14.30	STEVENAGE	10	ON TIME
14.55	LEEDS	18	ON TIME

Write the name of your destination here:

____

Capital work, detective! Now quickly buy a ticket and board the carriage behind the suspect.

Answer on page 112

Task 24: The Stuff of Legend

An infamous gang of thieves, the Slippery Eels, have their sights set on stealing some of the world's most legendary treasures. What they don't know is that the net is closing in on them!

Crack this next code to find out the names of four priceless artefacts the gang want to get their mitts on.

Key:

	1	2	3	4	5
1	A	B	C	D	E
2	F	G	H	I	J
3	K	L	M	N	O
4	P	Q	R	S	T
5	U	V	W	X	Y/Z

Example: 31, 15, 14 would make the word CUP.

HARTIGAN'S HINT: Move horizontally along the row to find the first digit, then vertically for the second.

A. 44, 35, 53, 34, 41 53, 12

__ __ __ __ __ __ __

41, 51, 44, 54, 42, 43, 55

__ __ __ __ __ __ __

B. 32, 53, 23, 55 22, 34, 11, 42, 23

__ __ __ __ __ __ __ __ __

C. 41, 42, 11, 33, 53, 43, 41

__ __ __ __ __ __ __

44, 13, 15, 23, 23

__ __ __ __ __

D. 44, 11, 43, 54, 11

__ __ __ __ __

33, 11, 34, 22, 11, 34, 42, 54, 11

__ __ __ __ __ __ __ __ __

14, 51, 11, 34, 23

__ __ __ __ __

Answer on page 112

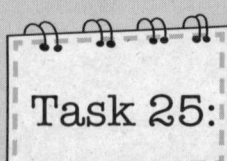

Task 25: Searching for Clues

Evidence may be collected in the unlikeliest of places, so make it a habit to leave no stone unturned in your investigations.

The word CLUE is written in the letter grid below three times. It may appear forwards, backwards, up, down or diagonally. Find it thrice!

		C	E	L	U		
C	U	L	L	L	C	U	U
C	L	C	U	U	E	U	C
L	E	E	C	L	E	E	L
U	C	U	E	U	L	C	U
L	L	C	L	U	C	U	U
		C	L	U	E		

Of course you found the clues, was it ever in doubt? I think not! This time work out which of these words cannot be rearranged to spell DETECTIVE.

Answer here:

Answers on pages 112 and 113

Task 26: Kid's Play

Here's one to get your little grey cells whirring . . . You find yourself in an empty room, save for a safe in the wall.

The room is completely bare – no furniture, curtains or carpet. Then you notice a piece of paper, sticking out between the floorboards.

Curious, you unfold the paper. At first glance, it appears to be a child's drawing. Appearances, as any detective worth their salt knows, can be deceptive! Could this crayoned creation be concealing a code?

HARTIGAN'S HINT: Read from left to right on the top row and then the bottom row.

Enter the 4-digit code here:

Answer on page 113

Task 27: Night Bites

Following a string of vicious attacks at a campsite, the agency has been tasked with tracking down a demonic nocturnal marsupial. I hope you've had your jabs! Fill in the missing letters of these spy-related words to reveal the name of our next mission.

C □ V E R T

S □ Y

A G □ N T

U N D E □ C O V E R

H □ C K E R

S E C R E □

C □ P H E R

D E A D D R □ P

E S P I O □ A G E

Answer on page 113

☐ U R N E D

C L ☐ S S I F I E D

E ☐ C R Y P T

C O ☐ E

A L ☐ A S

☐ O V E R

M ☐ R S E C O D E

M ☐ L E

S ☐ A K E O U T

Our next mission will be:

___ ___ ___ ___ ___ ___ ___ ___ ___

___ ___ ___ ___ ___ ___ ___ ___ ___

HARTIGAN'S HINT: Progress isn't a straight line – complete the words you know first then come back to any that prove trickier.

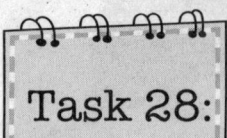

Task 28: Top-secret Test

Morse code is a cipher that consists of dots and dashes when written down, and long and short clicks when messages are sent over the radio waves. I rather rely on this method of communication when digital technologies have been compromised.

Made up of three dots, three dashes and three more dots, the letters SOS were chosen as an easy distress signal to remember and send quickly.

S O S

··· – – – ···

A	·–	J	·– – –	S	···
B	–···	K	–·–	T	–
C	–·–·	L	·–··	U	··–
D	–··	M	– –	V	···–
E	·	N	–·	W	·– –
F	··–·	O	– – –	X	–··–
G	– –·	P	·– –·	Y	–·– –
H	····	Q	– –·–	Z	– – ··
I	··	R	·–·		

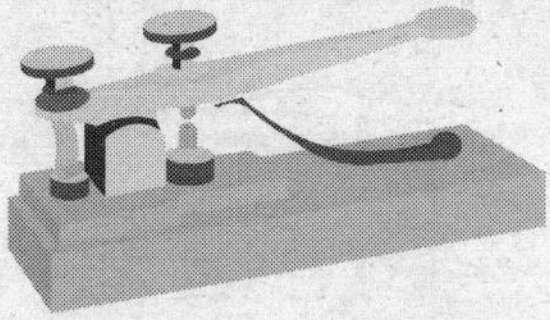

Decipher the spy-related words written in top-secret Morse code below.

1. ... . –.–. .–. . –

Answer: ___ ___ ___ ___ ___ ___

2. – –. .– –.. – –. . –

Answer: ___ ___ ___ ___ ___ ___

3. – – .. .. – – – –.

Answer: ___ ___ ___ ___ ___ ___ ___

4. .– – –. . –. –

Answer: ___ ___ ___ ___ ___

Answer on page 113

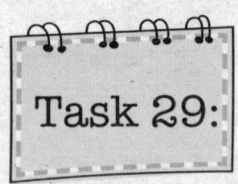

Task 29: Whose Shoes?

Six fresh footprint samples were taken at the scene of an attempted robbery at the famed Saveloy's Sausage Factory. Disturbed by the guard dog, Banger, the suspects fled with nothing. Zilch. Not a sausage.

Not half an hour later the hapless (and hungry) half-dozen were picked up by police in the nearest pub, the Sneak Inn.

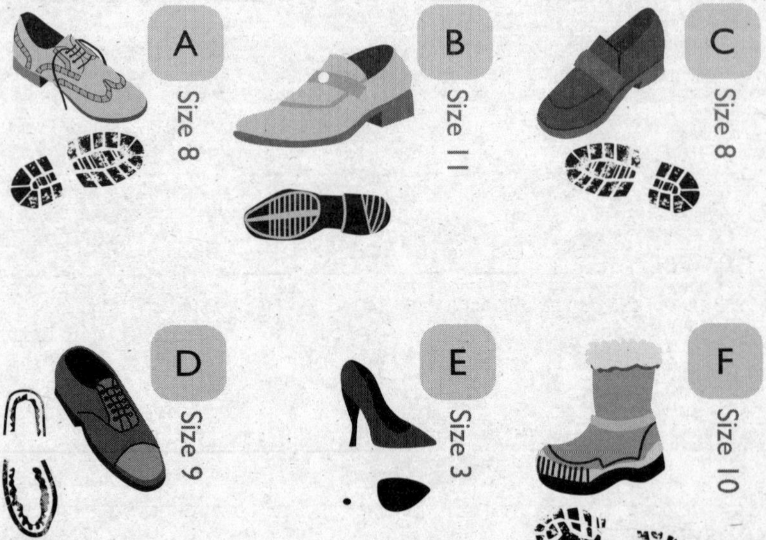

Read the descriptions, then study the shoes to match them to their owners. Write your answers in the boxes below.

1. Anonymous Aubrey wears lace-up shoes and is light on his feet.

2. Burglar Brad wears winter boots all year round.

3. Crooked Camilla would not be seen dead in flats. Standing at a tiny 150 cm tall, she needs the height!

4. Devious Dev is a dapper fellow, who prefers slip-on shoes cobbled in Italy.

5. Evil Emerick likes loafers too and has rather large feet.

6. Fabio Felon has the same size feet as Dev, but will only wear shoes with laces.

Answer on page 114

Task 30: Making Shapes

From what I've witnessed so far, you're shaping up to be quite the promising agent. Allow yourself a little victory dance . . . I won't judge!

The next task requires you to reveal a secret message. Every shape in the code key stands for one letter of the alphabet. Fill in the answer by writing the matching letter above each shape.

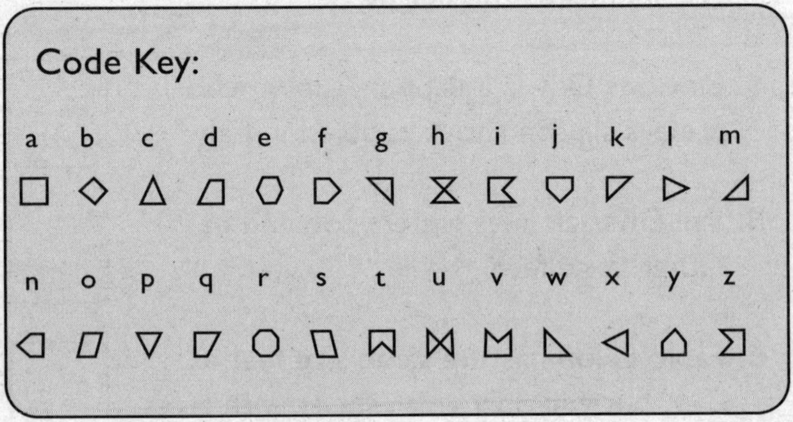

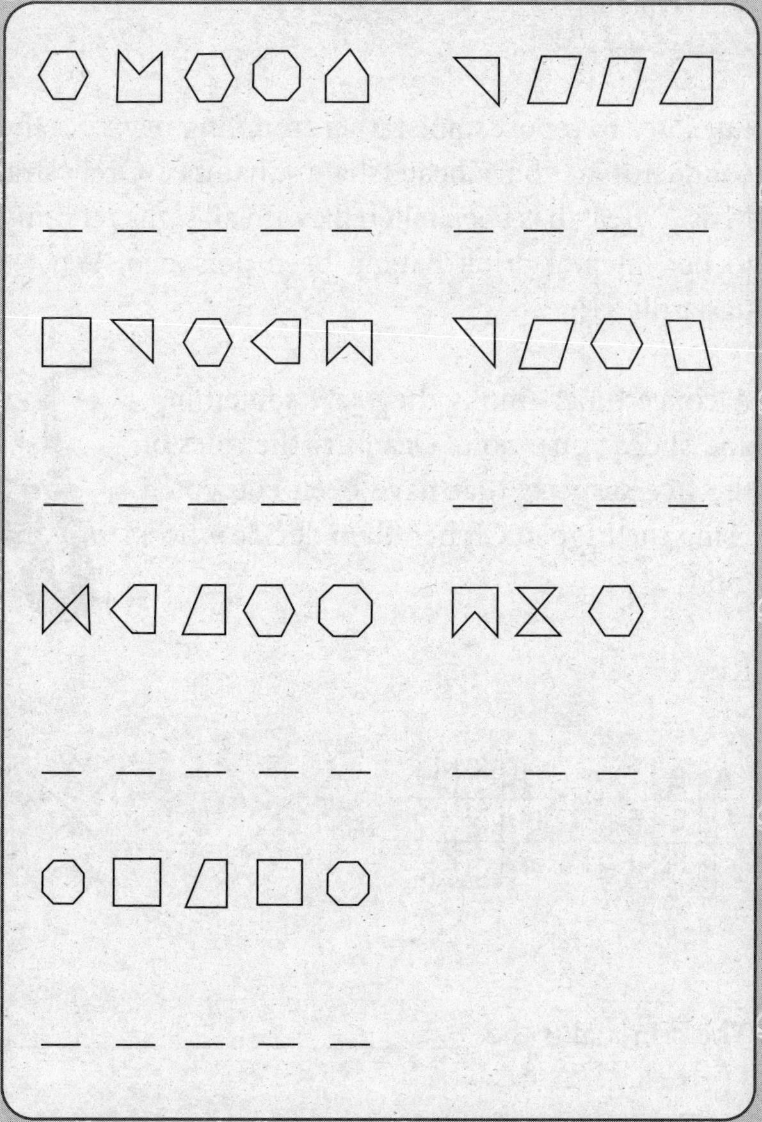

Answer on page 114

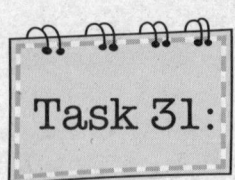

Task 31: Foul Play

I'm sorry to report some rather troubling news . . . the conductor of the Cheatersham Chamber Orchestra, Miss A. Beat, has been taken ill, with all signs pointing to her interval drink having been poisoned. What a dastardly crime!

A concertgoer thinks they saw something, and slides you a note. Decipher the roles of the five suspects that have been encrypted using the Pigpen Cipher, then decide who's guilty.

Key:

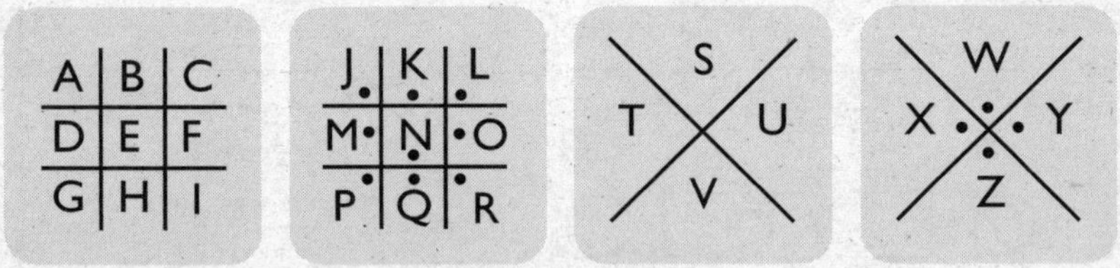

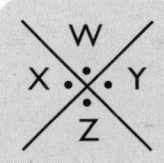

The criminal is the: ______________________

Answer on page 114

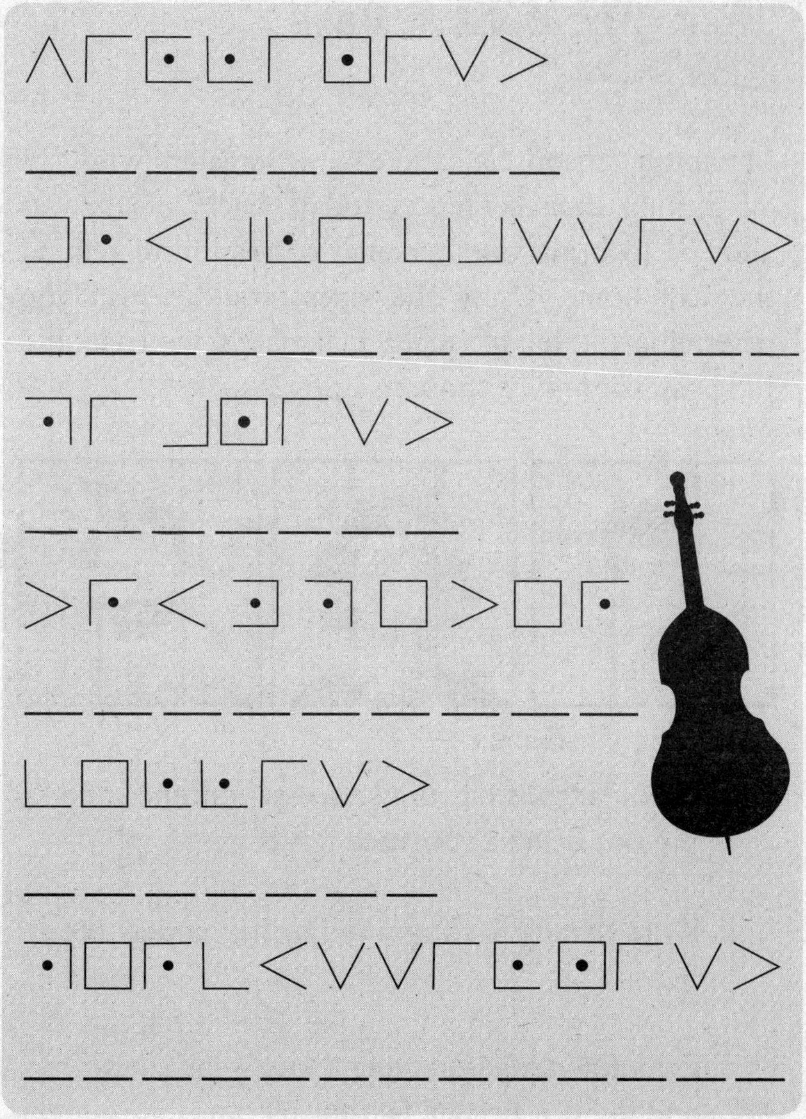

HARTIGAN'S HINT: The culprit is somehow different from their five fellow musicians. Look carefully at the beginning, middle and end of each name.

Task 32: Behind Bars

Plumpton Prison has three new inmates, who are all starting their sentences today. Each inmate was allowed to bring one personal possession to remind them of home. Using the clues provided, can you determine the length of each inmate's sentence and the possession they chose to bring?

1. Max Margolis has the shortest sentence and did not bring a romance novel

2. Kylie Kwang is comforted by her cuddly teddy bear

3. Edna Edwards is serving a four-year sentence and did not bring a feather pillow

Complete the grid by adding ticks and crosses.

<table>
<tr><td colspan="2" rowspan="2"></td><th colspan="3">Sentence</th><th colspan="3">Personal Item</th></tr>
<tr><th>3 years</th><th>4 years</th><th>5 years</th><th>pillow</th><th>teddy</th><th>book</th></tr>
<tr><th rowspan="3">Suspect</th><th>Max Margolis</th><td></td><td></td><td></td><td></td><td></td><td></td></tr>
<tr><th>Kylie Kwang</th><td></td><td></td><td></td><td></td><td></td><td></td></tr>
<tr><th>Edna Edwards</th><td></td><td></td><td></td><td></td><td></td><td></td></tr>
<tr><th rowspan="3">Personal Item</th><th>pillow</th><td></td><td></td><td></td></tr>
<tr><th>teddy</th><td></td><td></td><td></td></tr>
<tr><th>book</th><td></td><td></td><td></td></tr>
</table>

Answer on page 115

Task 33: SIM-ilar Sight

On we go! Your detective skills are getting stronger with every task. In a box of evidence, there are nine SIM cards. One of these was extracted from the phone of a foolhardy fraudster wanted in connection with a series of scandalous scams.

The cards look much alike. To find the swindler's SIM, follow my rules on the next page.

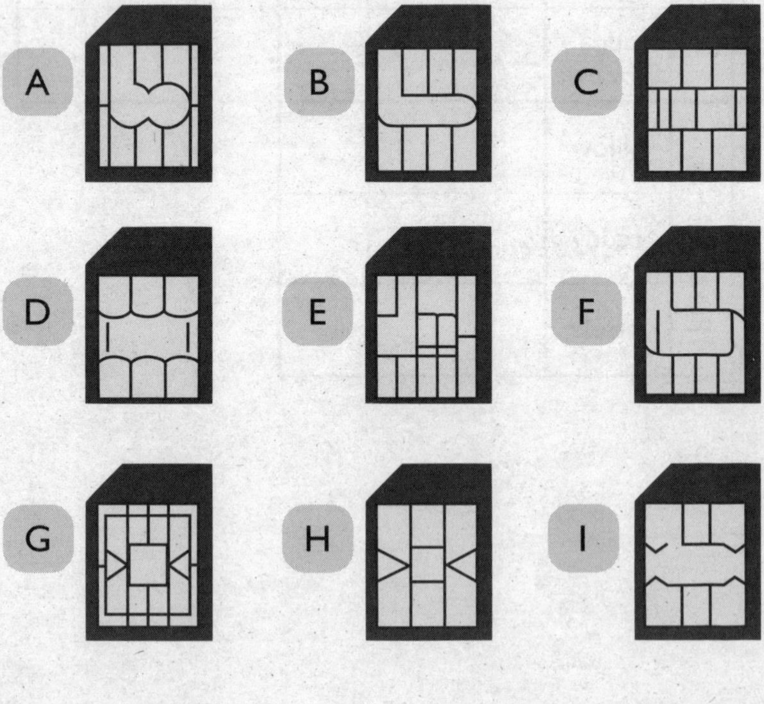

Rules:

The design of the small chip inside the outer casing:

- is symmetrical
- has lines that all join another line
- has no curved lines
- contains four different shapes (shapes may be repeated and/or flipped)

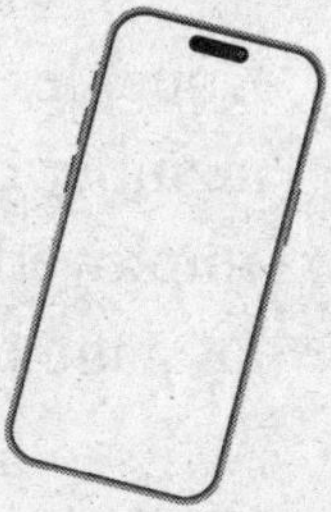

Draw it here and write the letter:

Answer:

Answer on page 115

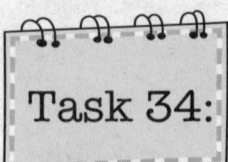

Task 34: Suitcase Scam

Knuckles Knutsen is a mole working undercover as a member of the infamous Greasby Gang. He has been employed to help put an end to a scam to steal guests' luggage from a five-star hotel.

Knuckles has just shared a postcard. You take a look. To the untrained eye, it doesn't tell us much, but on closer inspection, you see that Knuckles has drawn tiny dots above some of the letters. Might they form some kind of secret code?

Dear Granny,
It's tropical out here! I'm
loving every second! Sun tan is
coming on already! Yesterday
was the best - happily eating
really delicious ice cream!
Love, Knuckles

Rewrite Knuckles' postcard here, copying only the letters with dots above them to reveal the name of the brains behind the suitcase scam.

___ ___ ___ ___ ___ ___ ___ ___ ___

___ ___ ___ ___   ___ ___ ___

___ ___ ___ ___ ___

HARTIGAN'S HINT: Work in pencil, so you can rub out any mistakes. Spacing out the letters a little will make it easier to organize them into words.

Answer on page 116

Task 35: Diamond Geezer

A jewellery heist has taken place at Sparkovski's flagship store. Witnesses report that the suspect made off with an enormous diamond in broad daylight! His smart attire – a three-piece suit and Italian brogues – had everyone fooled.

The witnesses tell you that the robber headed east. Make your way through the diamond maze to follow him passing only even numbers.

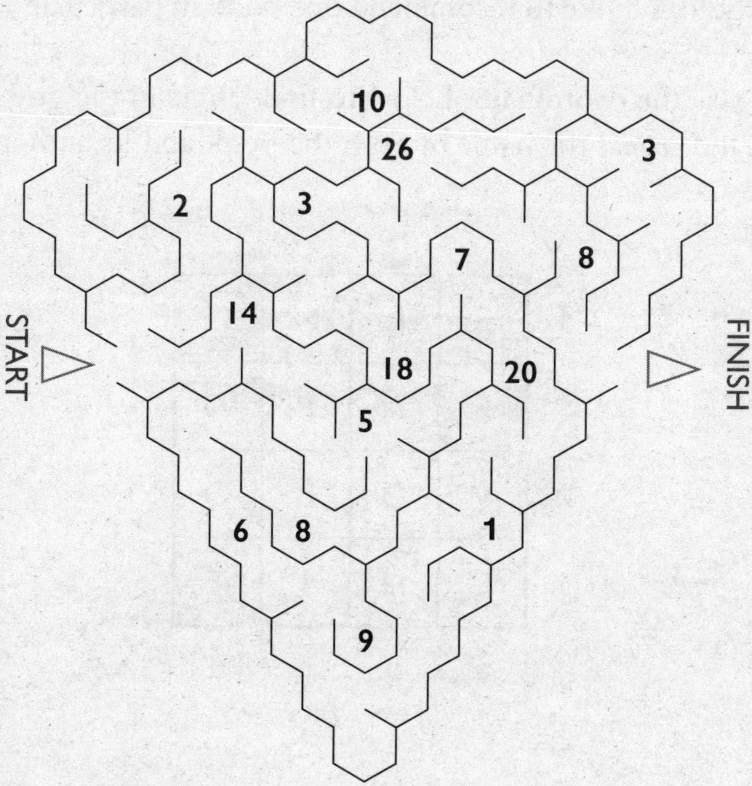

Answer on page 116

Task 36: Library Loan

Make the city's public library the next stop on your mission to becoming a super sleuth! If I may be so bold, I'd like to recommend one book in particular. . .

Use the coordinates below to find letters in the grid, and reveal the name of both the book and its author.

Y					
4	S	R	N	G	
3	E	A	P	W	
2	V	D	B	O	
1	C	H	I	T	
	a	b	c	d	X

HARTIGAN'S HINT: Read the x axis, then the y axis.

b1, d2, d3 d1, d2

___ ___ ___ ___ ___

c2, a3 b3 d1, d2, c3

___ ___ ___ ___ ___ ___

b2, a3, d1, a3, a1, d1, c1, a2, a3

___ ___ ___ ___ ___ ___ ___ ___ ___

BY

b1, b3, b4, d1, c1, d4, b3, c4

___ ___ ___ ___ ___ ___ ___ ___

c2, b4, d2, d3, c4, a3

___ ___ ___ ___ ___ ___

Answer on page 116

Task 37: Locked Out

Your next investigation leads you to an abandoned church, following reports of a fight inside. *Gulp!*

You rattle the handle to discover the door is locked.

Six keys hang on the wall in the church porch. One of them must surely fit the lock, but which? Locate the correct key as swiftly as you can.

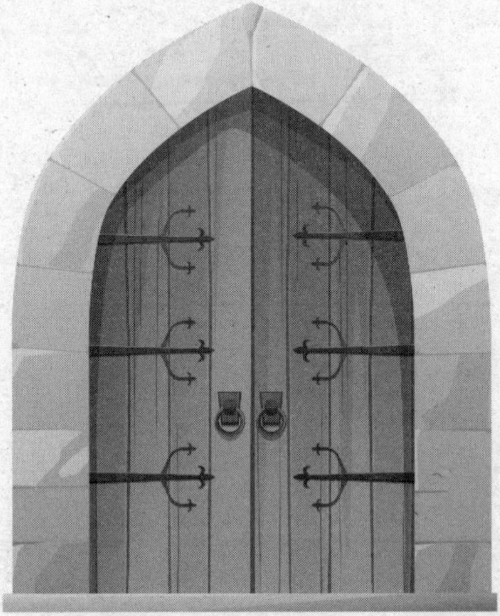

Which key fits in this lock?

Write your answer here: ___________

Answer on page 117

Task 38: Restaurant Rivals

Today's task is to track down the location of a safe, hidden somewhere in the home of Chef Stéphanie Soupçon. A second chef, Serge Saveur, accuses fierce rival Soupçon of having stolen his recipe book after security cameras caught her sneaking out of his kitchen in the dead of night.

I'm pinging you a plan of the building, along with some coded instructions. Let's see whether just desserts are about to be served.

Key:

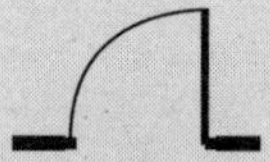
door

window

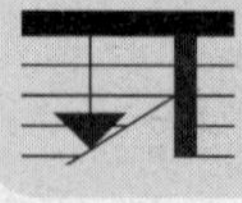
stairs

The room with the safe:

- has only one door
- has one or more windows
- does not have any stairs
- has two external (outer) walls
- is square-shaped

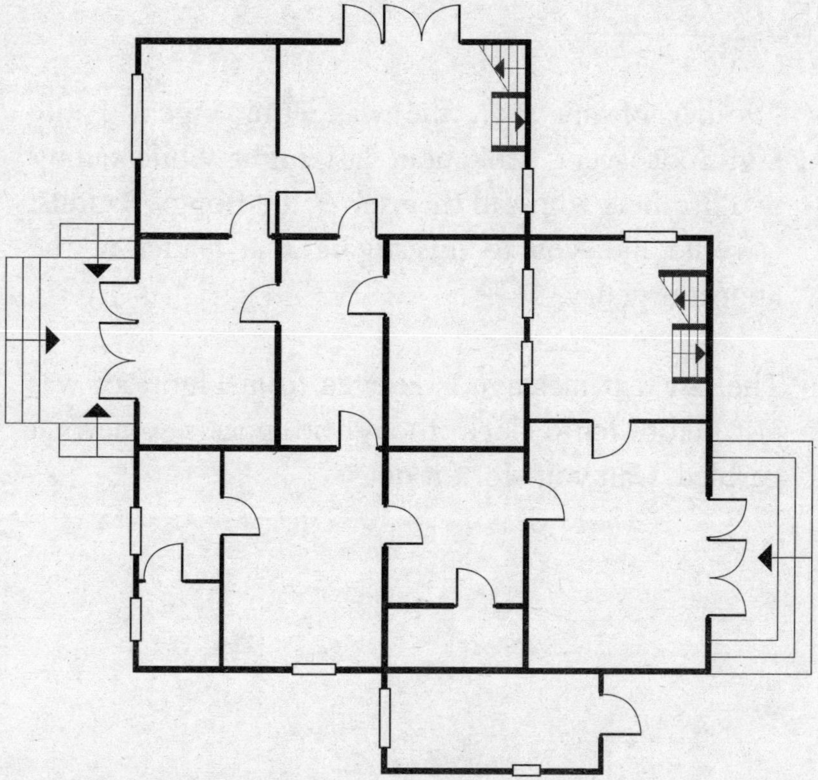

Circle the room where you believe the safe to be.

HARTIGAN'S HINT: Cross out the wrong rooms as you rule them out.

Answer on page 117

Task 39: Missing in Action

Another of my staff, the wandering Agent Pattie Lightfoot, went walkabout last night while tailing two brothers who call themselves the Boggy Bandits. I would like you to investigate as a matter of the utmost urgency.

The last text message I received from Lightfoot was just before ten o'clock, though it appears somewhat garbled. Can you work it out?

HARTIGAN'S HINT: Think about the type of letters that are missing.

H__RT__G__N! __'M

L__CK__D __N TH__

P__BL__C T__ __L__TS

__T __C__RN P__RK.

TH__Y TR__ __D T__

FL__SH MY PH__NE

D__WN TH__

T__ __L__T! __F Y__ __

G__T TH__S M__SS__G__,

S__ND H__LP!

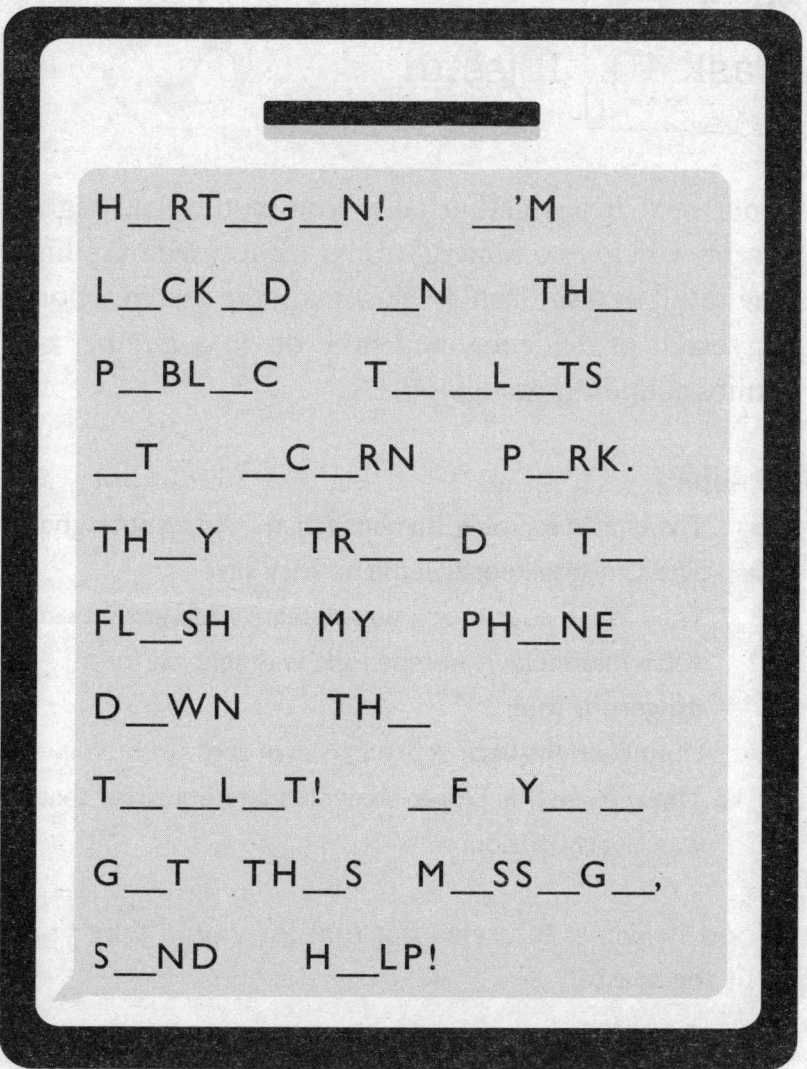

Sterling stuff, young agent. Head there now, before you get caught short!

Answer on page 118

Task 40: Rigged!

Your next investigation takes you to the Arkwright Arena, where two football teams are accused of fixing the result of a big match! You study the match report in search of evidence, and note down a number of guilty-sounding goings-on.

Minute:

15 The United forward, number ten, missed an open goal.

20 The City goalkeeper let in an easy save.

46 The United coach took off the team's top goalscorer.

60 A City midfielder, number six, was sent off for a dangerous foul.

77 United's right-back scored an own goal.

90+6 The referee, Mr Dupe, allowed a late equalizer that was clearly offside!

Good heavens! Interviewing that lot would take you half the season!

Then you receive an anonymous note, encoded using the Fence Cipher! Someone wants to rid the beautiful game of its bad eggs while keeping their identity under wraps! Use the Fence Cipher to decode the message:

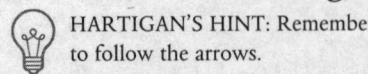

HARTIGAN'S HINT: Remember to follow the arrows.

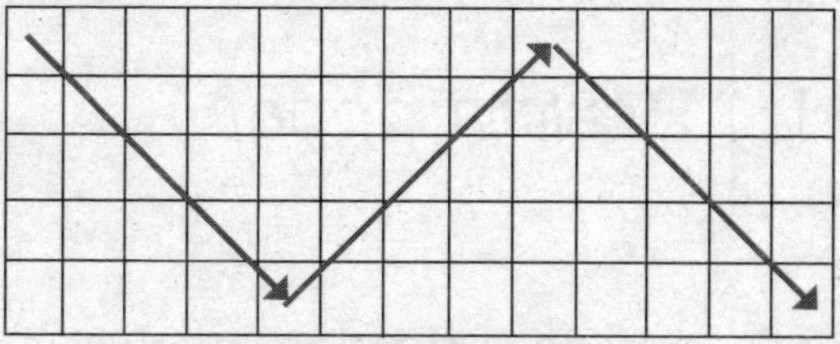

C	O	R	N	E	R	C	H	E	A	T	E	R
H	I	C	R	O	S	S	B	A	R	F	A	N
N	E	T	D	U	M	M	Y	P	O	S	T	S
C	I	T	Y	F	U	N	C	O	M	M	I	T
K	I	T	A	N	G	L	E	R	O	L	L	X

Write the answer here: ____ _______ ___

It appears the above person wasn't acting alone – another participant was showing less than sportspersonlike qualities! Translate this second cipher:

R	I	G	H	T	H	I	T	R	O	P	H	Y
B	E	L	I	E	V	E	M	U	D	C	U	P
O	F	F	S	I	D	E	T	O	R	U	N	S
C	H	E	E	R	E	N	D	S	L	I	P	S
W	I	N	F	R	E	E	K	I	C	K	M	E

Write the answer here: ________ __ ____

Answer on page 118

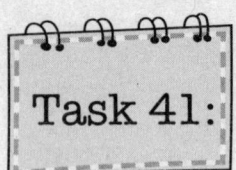

Task 41: Heartstopper

The Agency's latest investigation involves a romance swindler, who uses fake online profiles to befriend the rich and lonely . . . before taking them to the cleaners!

When you interview the victims, they all describe women of a very similar appearance.

Upon further investigation, it seems the swindler has become sloppy – one time she forgot to use a false name! When you search the HBDA database for 'Miss Greta Grime', the system links her to an alarming number of cases.

Just how many hearts might the sneaky suspect have broken? Find all the times the word **GRIME** appears in the grid below. It can be spotted reading forwards, backwards, up, down and diagonally.

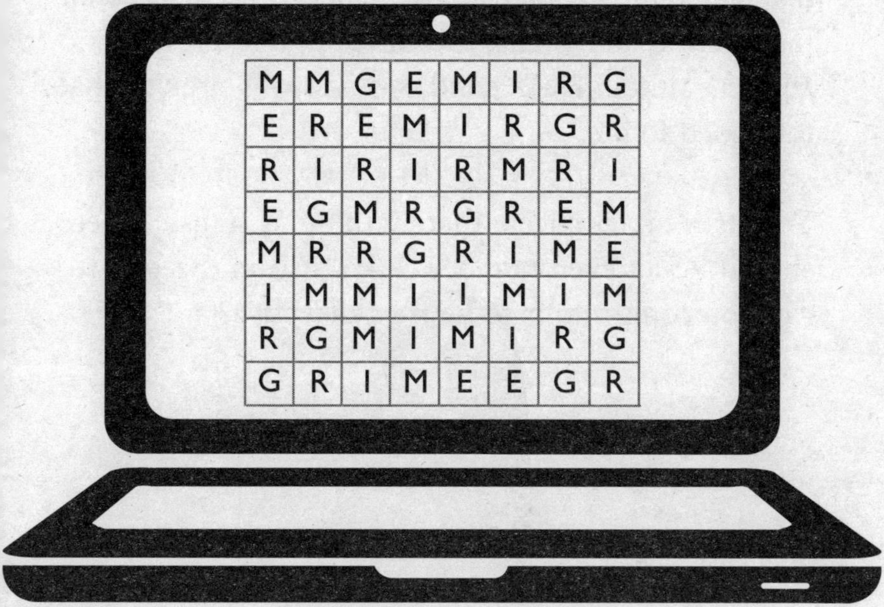

M	M	G	E	M	I	R	G
E	R	E	M	I	R	G	R
R	I	R	I	R	M	R	I
E	G	M	R	G	R	E	M
M	R	R	G	R	I	M	E
I	M	M	I	I	M	I	M
R	G	M	I	M	I	R	G
G	R	I	M	E	E	G	R

Write your answer here:

Answer on page 119

Task 42: Something Fishy

You are called to the garden of a perplexed pensioner, Mr Marsh, who is convinced he heard fish rustlers in his garden the previous night. When he went to count his prized shoal of koi, they all appeared present and correct, although he confesses his eyes aren't what they used to be.

You'll need to check that nothing is amiss. There should be an even number of koi fish in the pond – can you confirm this to be true, detective?

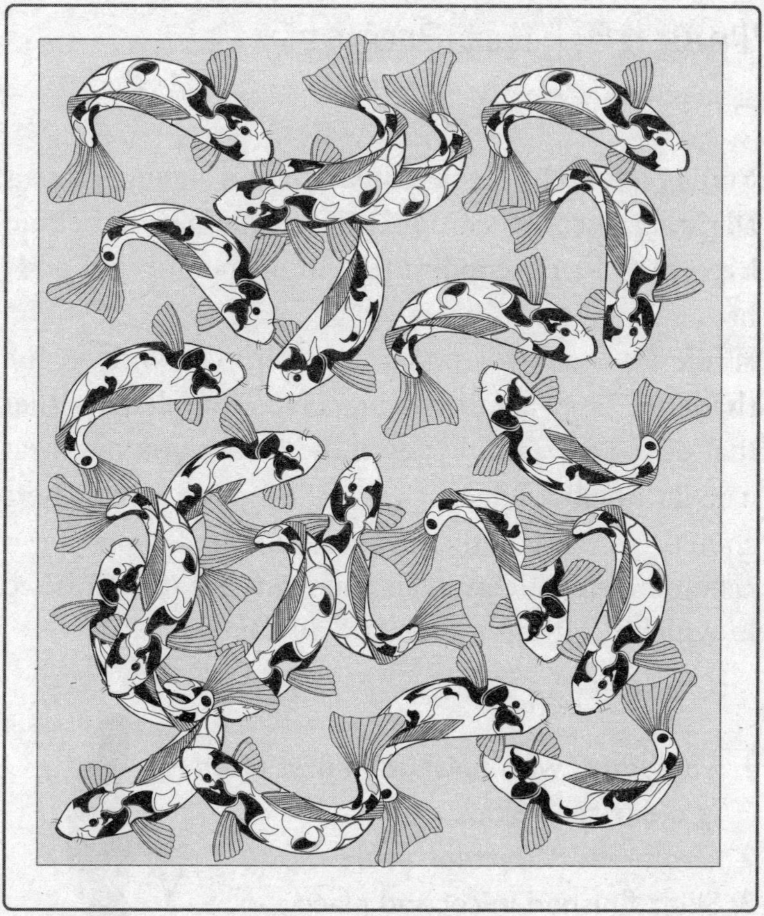

Write the number here: ☐

Has a theft occurred? Yes ☐ No ☐

Answer on page 119

Task 43: Hot Property

In the park at dusk you stumble across a gang of teens all riding e-scooters. Could these be the culprits behind a recent spate of scooter thefts in the neighbourhood?

While you wait for police back-up, you lurk in the shadows. They are discussing a race completed earlier that day. You scribble down the details you overhear in your notebook.

Using the clues below, can you work out who finished in which position in their rowdy race?

1. The youth who finished in first place is older than Skidz.
2. Grommet is thirteen years old.
3. Skidz finished in second place.
4. Bunny is one year younger than the racer who finished third.
5. Fakie is the oldest.

Complete the grid by adding ticks and crosses.

		Age				Position			
		13	14	15	16	1st	2nd	3rd	4th
Suspect	Bunny								
	Fakie								
	Skidz								
	Grommet								
Position	1st								
	2nd								
	3rd								
	4th								

HARTIGAN'S HINT: Study each clue carefully. It may contain a number of pieces of information.

Answer on page 120

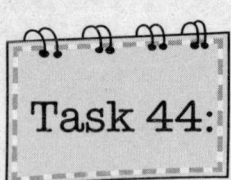

Task 44: Smugglers' Run

In an old smugglers' tunnel, a trove of pirate treasure, thought to belong to one Captain Codswallop, has been uncovered. Take stock of the valuables by placing them in a crate.

You must fill the grid so that there is one of each of the following pieces of treasure in each row, column and mini grid.

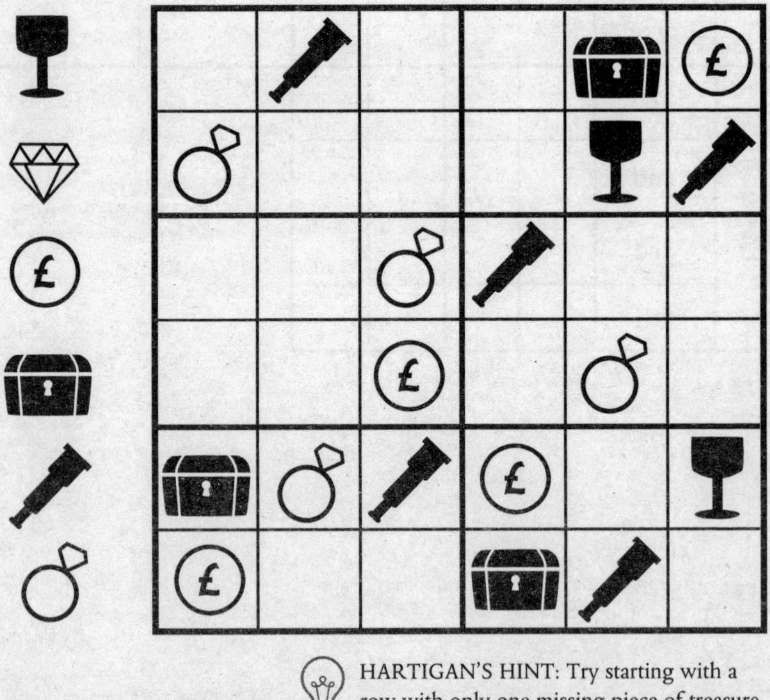

HARTIGAN'S HINT: Try starting with a row with only one missing piece of treasure.

One item of treasure is worth more than the rest put together. Fill in the missing letters, then unscramble the word they spell to reveal the priceless treasure.

1. R U _ Y
2. C _ I N
3. C H E S _
4. T E _ E S C O P _
5. R I N _

The treasure is: _ _ _ _ _ _

Answer on page 121

Task 45: Play the Game

Lowdown crew the Groundhog Gang have planned a big job in town. It's our job to stop them! Rather helpfully, they have left a coded message at the Darts Club detailing their target.

It was meant for their blaster, who is out fetching supplies of dynamite, but you arrive first!

Each number on the dartboard corresponds to a letter, although not every letter in the alphabet is represented. Below is a partial key that you should be able to complete without too much trouble. Then you can decode the numbers on the dartboards.

Key:

1	2	3	4	5	6	7	8	9	10
	S	R		P		N		L	

11	12	13	14	15	16	17	18	19	20
J		H			E	D			A

Answer on page 122

1

Letters:

☐ ☐ ☐

2

Letters:

☐ ☐ ☐

3

Letters:

☐ ☐ ☐

You should have nine letters in total. Reorganize the letters to reveal the gang's next target.

Answer: __ __ __ __ __   __ __ __ __

HARTIGAN'S HINT: Forget about the final six letters of the alphabet – they are not included in the puzzle.

Task 46: Patchwork Puzzler

Don't worry, young agent. Not too many more cases to crack remain. Soon you can put your feet up, I promise. Which begs the question, what does an HBDA agent do when it's time for bed?

Complete the key, then study the hidden message on my quaint but cosy quilt.

Key:

A	B	C	D	E	F	G	H	I	J	K	L	M
	25							18				

N	O	P	Q	R	S	T	U	V	W	X	Y	Z
		11			8	7				3		

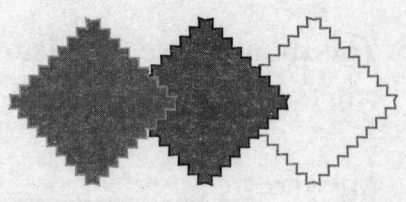

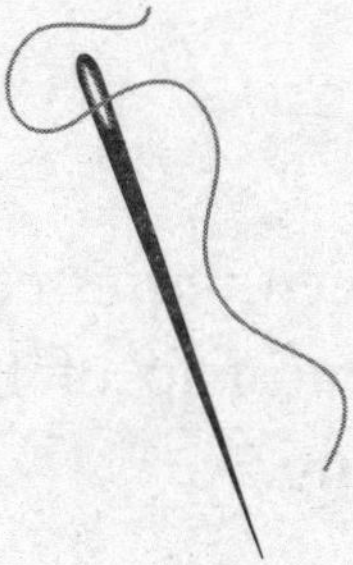

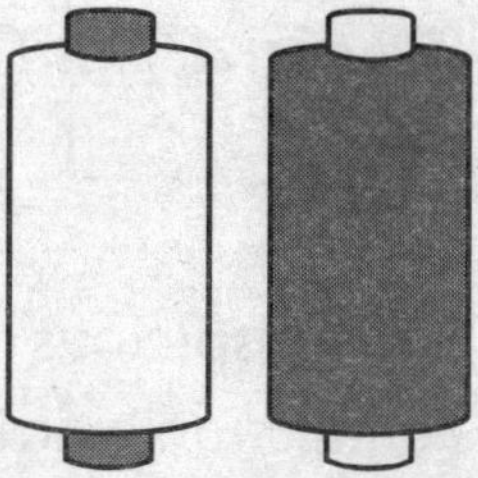

Answer: ___ ___ ___ ___   ___ ___

___ ___ ___ ___ ___ ___ ___ ___ ___ ___!

Answer on page 122

Task 47: Guilty Party

Six suspicious suspects have been arrested in connection with a robbery – the pup-nap of Dame van Ditzy's pampered pooch, Pudding.

Now you must prove who's guilty of pinching the pup. The suspects' statements are below. Lie-detector tests confirm that **exactly four** of the suspects each told **one lie**, and their other two statements were true.

Using evidence below, can you confirm the guilty party?

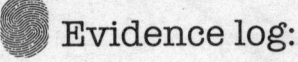

Evidence log:

HARTIGAN'S HINT: Keep a close eye on the suspect that is mentioned the most times.

Arnold Angel said:

- It wasn't Bjorn Bent.
- It wasn't Davey D. Dodge.
- It wasn't Eyeball Earl.

Bjorn Bent said:

- It wasn't Arnold Angel.
- It wasn't Clara LeCheat.
- It wasn't Eyeball Earl.

Clara LeCheat said:

- It wasn't Bjorn Bent.
- It wasn't Eyeball Earl.
- It wasn't Fingers McFilch.

Davey Diamond said:

- It wasn't Arnold Angel.
- It wasn't Clara LeCheat.
- It wasn't Fingers McFilch.

Eyeball Earl said:

- It wasn't Clara LeCheat.
- It wasn't Davey D. Dodge.
- It wasn't Fingers McFilch.

Fingers McFilch said:

- It wasn't Arnold Angel.
- It wasn't Clara LeCheat.
- It wasn't Davey D. Dodge.

Write your answer here: ______________________________

Answer on page 123

Task 48: Where Next?

The HBDA database throws up another interesting snippet regarding a suspect peddling counterfeit cosmetics.

Queenie Le Chic has been spotted at the same location at the same time for the past three weeks running. Just twenty minutes remain until this week's appointment . . . you'll need to get a wiggle on if you're to catch a crook!

Crack my code to reveal the location.

HARTIGAN'S HINT: The beginning is a good place to start.

Because of your

Exceptional work

A number of criminals are

Under lock and key.

That's thanks to you!

You are doing brilliantly, young detective.

So, keep going on your quest.

Above all else, be careful,

Lest the suspect is dangerous.

Only try your best

Not to let them escape!

Write your answer here:

___ ___ ___ ___ ___ ___   ___ ___ ___ ___ ___

That's some dazzling detective work!

Answer on page 124

Task 49: PIN Problem

You're well on your way to becoming a fine detective, so I've decided to issue you with an agency laptop and a celebratory smoothie slightly ahead of schedule.

To access the computer, you'll need to work out the 4-digit PIN that I've set. Think carefully as you slurp on your fruity drink – entering the wrong number three times will lock you out for good.

Clues:

The first digit is an even number that can be divided equally by 2.

The second digit is double the first.

The third digit is one less than the first.

The fourth digit is the sum of the first three numbers.

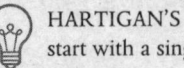

HARTIGAN'S HINT: Make sure you start with a single-digit number.

Attempt 1:

Attempt 2:

Attempt 3:

Answer on page 124

Task 50: Closing the Book

Well, this is a turn-up for the books – your final task is to crack the Book Cipher! You'll need to look back through this puzzling paperback to work out a message that I've cunningly hidden in its pages.

Here's how the Book Cipher works . . .

Example:

To find the word that is encoded 3-1-1

- turn to page 3
- look at the first line
- find the first word, which is 'splendid'!

20–2–4   6–6–3,   29–1–2!

__________   __________,   __________!

4–1–9   1–15–3

__________   __________

14–1–7   4–4–2!

__________   __________!

HARTIGAN'S HINT: Hyphenated words count as one word!

A thousand congratulations! You've earned your very own badge! Your training is complete . . . you're now a fully fledged member of the Hartigan Browne Detective Agency! I expect this badge will serve you well on many more missions to come.

Agent

NAME:________________________________

Answer on page 124

ANSWERS

Task 1: In a Pickle

From page 2

1. CUCUMBER
2. EGGS
3. PEPPERS
4. BEETROOT
5. CABBAGES
6. ONIONS

Hartigan's perfect pickle: **PEPPERS**

Task 2: Number Crunching

From page 4

3	2	8	9	5	6	4	1	7
9	4	7	1	8	3	5	6	2
6	1	5	4	2	7	8	9	3
7	6	2	5	4	8	1	3	9
8	3	4	7	1	9	2	5	6
5	9	1	6	3	2	7	8	4
2	7	9	8	6	1	3	4	5
1	5	6	3	7	4	9	2	8
4	8	3	2	9	5	6	7	1

The 4-digit code is: **6749**

Task 3: Ride the Bus

From page 6

The correct bus route number is 73.

Task 4: On the Fence

From page 8

FOLLOW A RED CAR.
TAKE A BLACK CAB.

Task 5: Spare Key

From page 10

Key **G** is the odd one out.

Task 6: Out of Sight

From page 12

Route C: WAREHOUSE

Task 7: Play it Safe

From page 14

The code is: 1120

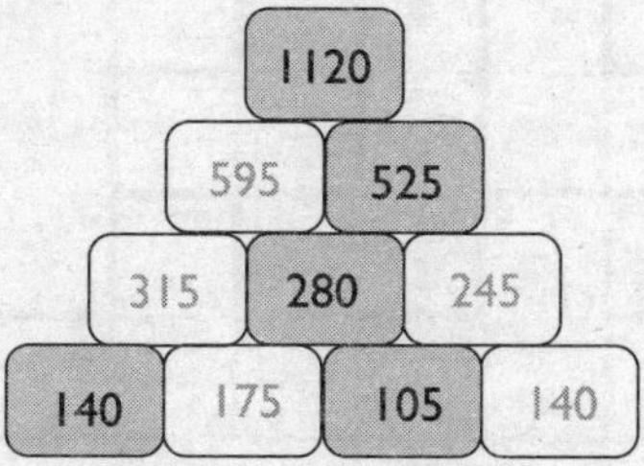

Task 8: Money Laundering

From page 16

There is £1,850 in total. (37 x £50)

Task 9: Dine and Dash

From page 18

Fingerprint A matches with number 3 (Barb Dwyer).
Fingerprint B matches with number 7 (Ivan Alilbi).

Task 10: Around the Block

From page 20

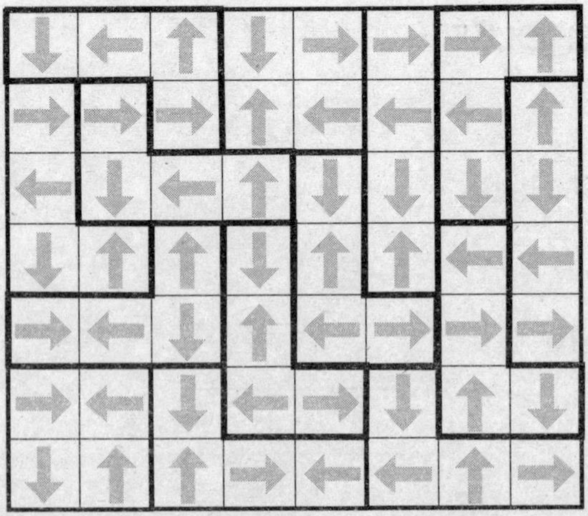

Task 11: Card Trick

From page 22

A.

B.

C.

D.

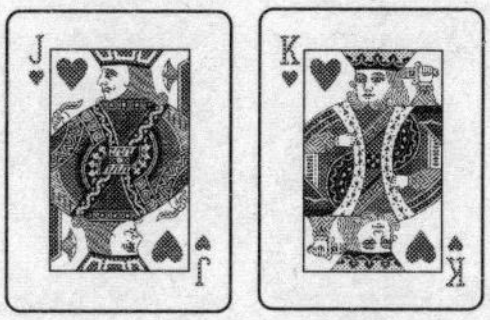

E.

Time: 9.25 **Suspect:** Jack King **Item:** A diamond

Task 12: Malicious Message

From page 24

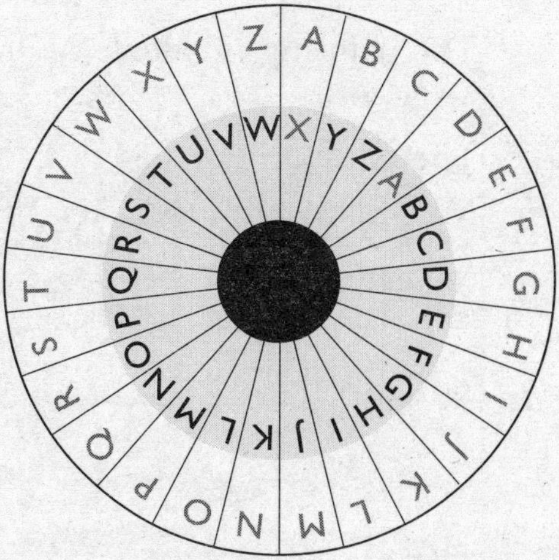

Cipher: This is a Caesar cipher with a shift of –3.

THIS IS A WARNING
TO STOP POKING
YOUR NOSE IN.
POKE AT YOUR
PERIL.

Task 13: Lucky for Some

From page 26

HOT CHOCOLATE	WATER
COFFEE	FLAPJACK
TEA	CAKE
ORANGE JUICE	COOKIE

£3.00	ORANGE JUICE
£1.95	COOKIE
= £4.95	

Task 14: In the Frame

From page 28

The painting is called: WOMAN IN BLACK

The museum is called:
MUSEUM OF FINE AND FANCY ART

Task 15: Subbing in

From page 30

6	4	7	1	6	6	4	9
4	7	5	6	2	3	7	0
1	8	9	3	4	1	8	4
0	6	4	9	7	0	**5**	3
6	3	6	4	**2**	**3**	**4**	6
4	6	8	1	9	3	6	5
7	5	2	3	5	4	9	7
0	6	1	8	6	4	8	9

Task 16: Data Breach

From page 32

		Suspect			Road Name			House Number		
		Mad Dog Doug	Wendy the Weasel	Baani Bander	Tinker Hill	Catcher Crescent	Mole Avenue	11	22	33
Door Colour	green	✔	✗	✗	✗	✗	✔	✗	✔	✗
	black	✗	✔	✗	✗	✔	✗	✔	✗	✗
	blue	✗	✗	✔	✔	✗	✗	✗	✗	✔
House Number	33	✗	✗	✔	✔	✗	✗			
	22	✔	✗	✗	✗	✗	✔			
	11	✗	✔	✗	✗	✔	✗			
Road Name	Mole Ave.	✔	✗	✗						
	Catcher Cres.	✗	✔	✗						
	Tinker Hill	✗	✗	✔						

Task 17: Planetary Problems

From page 34

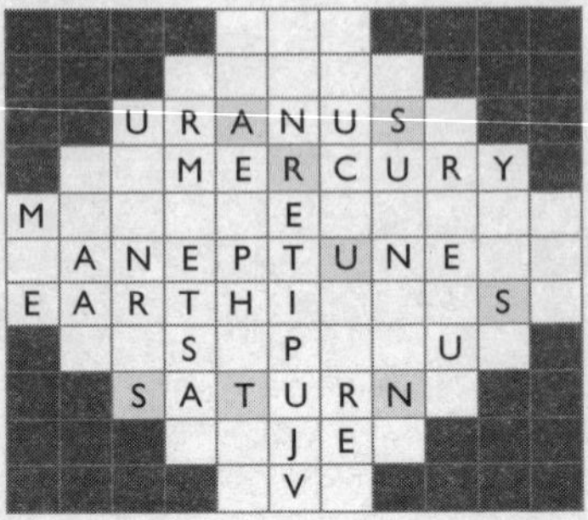

The stolen elements are: SUN, STARS

Task 18: Sneaker Scam

From page 36

MEET AT NINE PM OUTSIDE STATION

Task 19: Island Tour

From page 38

The delivery location is: H,3

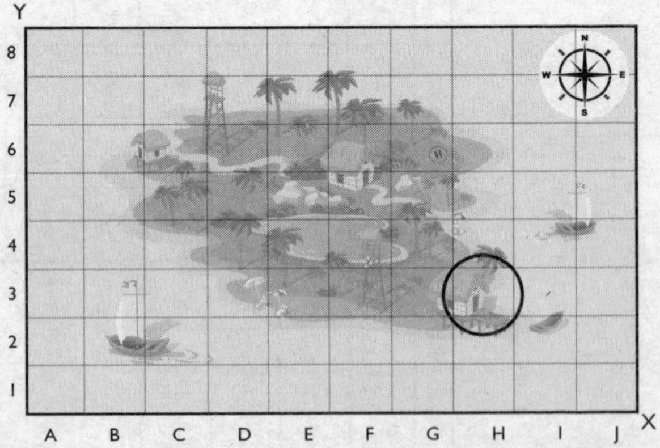

Task 20: Valuable Vase

From page 40

Piece D is the spare piece.

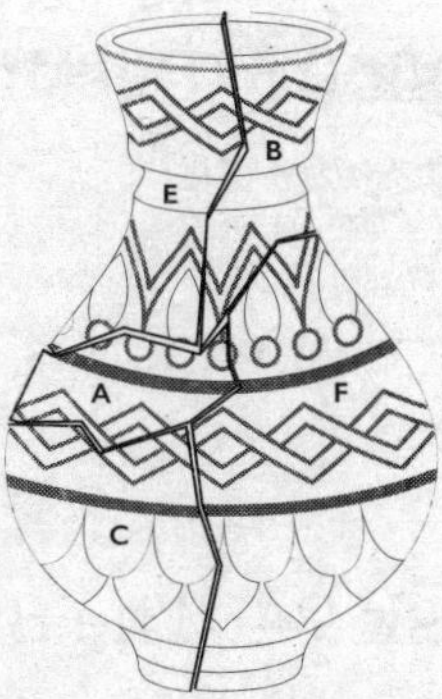

Task 21: Alpha Bravo Charlie

From page 42

1. HOTEL LIFT
2. PARK BENCH
3. BUS STOP
4. UNDER THE BRIDGE

Task 22: Seeing Double

From page 44

Silhouette **A** is the true Hartigan (me) – he's the only one with a beard.

The message reads: MEET ME UNDER THE VIADUCT AT MIDNIGHT. COME ALONE AND TELL NO ONE.

Task 23: Destination Unknown

From page 46

The destination is: CAMBRIDGE

Task 24: The Stuff of Legend

From page 48

1. SWORD OF DESTINY
2. HOLY GRAIL
3. DIAMOND SKULL
4. SANTA MARGARITA PEARL

Task 25: Searching for Clues

From page 50

		C	E	L	U		
C	U	L	**L**	L	C	U	U
C	L	C	U	**U**	E	U	C
L	E	E	C	L	**E**	E	L
U	C	U	**E**	**U**	**L**	**C**	U
L	L	C	L	U	C	U	U
		C	**L**	**U**	**E**		

The answer is **4.** DECEIVEDT cannot be rearranged to spell DETECTIVE.

Task 26: Kid's Play

From page 52

The 4-digit code is: 3 7 5 4

Task 27: Night Bites

From page 54

Our next mission is called:
OPERATION BANDICOOT

Task 28: Top-secret Test

From page 56

1. SECRET
2. GADGET
3. MISSION
4. AGENT

Task 29: Whose Shoes?

From page 58

1 = D	3 = E	5 = B
2 = F	4 = C	6 = A

Task 30: Making Shapes

From page 60

The message reads: EVERY GOOD AGENT GOES UNDER THE RADAR

Task 31: Foul Play

From page 62

1. violinist
2. double bassist
3. pianist
4. trumpeter
5. cellist
6. percussionist

The culprit is the trumpeter – the other musicians all end in -ist.

Task 32: Behind Bars

From page 64

		Sentence			Personal item		
		3 years	4 years	5 years	pillow	teddy	book
Suspect	Max Margolis	✔	✗	✗	✔	✗	✗
	Kylie Kwang	✗	✗	✔	✗	✔	✗
	Edna Edwards	✗	✔	✗	✗	✗	✔
Personal item	pillow	✔	✗	✗			
	teddy	✗	✗	✔			
	book	✗	✔	✗			

Task 33: A SIM-ilar Sight

From page 66

The SIM is: H

Task 34: Suitcase Scam

From page 68

The suspect is: TOOTHLESS TONY THE THIRD

Task 35: Diamond Geezer

From page 70

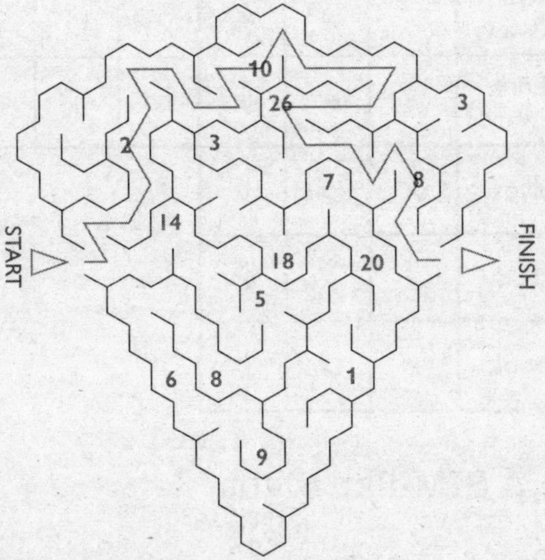

Task 36: Library Loan

From page 72

HOW TO BE A TOP DETECTIVE
BY HARTIGAN BROWNE

Task 37: Locked Out

From page 74

Correct key is C

Task 38: Restaurant Rivals

From page 76

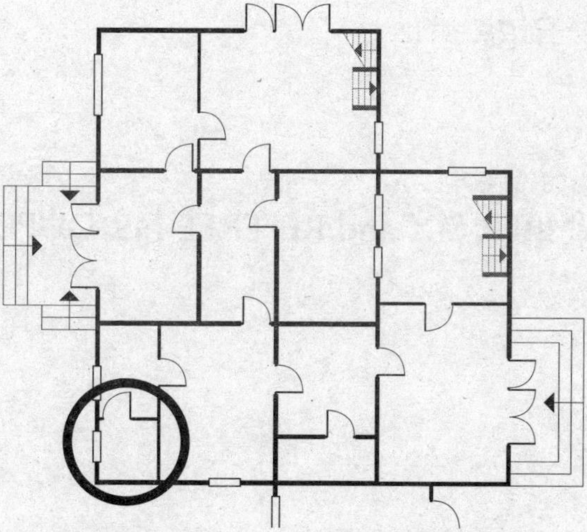

Task 39: Missing in Action

From page 78

The message reads:

HARTIGAN! I'M LOCKED IN THE PUBLIC TOILETS AT ACORN PARK. THEY TRIED TO FLUSH MY PHONE DOWN THE TOILET! IF YOU GET THIS MESSAGE, SEND HELP!

Task 40: Rigged!

From page 80

The culprits are:
CITY NUMBER SIX and REFEREE MR DUPE

Task 41: Heartstopper

From page 82

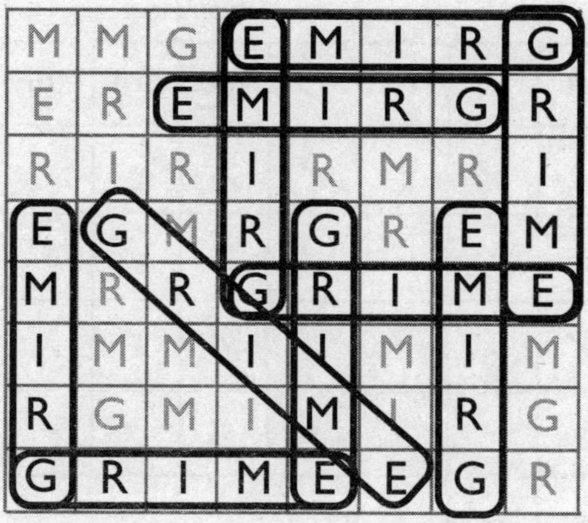

Answer: Greta Grime is likely guilty of 10 crimes.

Task 42: Something Fishy

From page 84

There are 21 koi in the pond – an odd number, which means a theft has indeed occurred!

Task 43: Hot Property

From page 86

		Age				Position			
		13	14	15	16	1st	2nd	3rd	4th
Suspect	Bunny	✗	✗	✔	✗	✔	✗	✗	✗
	Fakie	✗	✗	✗	✔	✗	✗	✔	✗
	Skidz	✗	✔	✗	✗	✗	✔	✗	✗
	Grommet	✔	✗	✗	✗	✗	✗	✗	✔
Position	1st	✗	✗	✔	✗				
	2nd	✗	✔	✗	✗				
	3rd	✗	✗	✗	✔				
	4th	✔	✗	✗	✗				

Task 44: Smugglers' Run

From page 88

1. RUBY
2. COIN
3. CHEST
4. TELESCOPE
5. RING

The treasure is: GOBLET

Task 45: Play the Game

From page 90

1	2	3	4	5	6	7	8	9	10
T	S	R	Q	P	O	N	M	L	K

11	12	13	14	15	16	17	18	19	20
J	I	H	G	F	E	D	C	B	A

The answer is: GREEN BANK

Task 46: Patchwork Puzzler

From page 92

A	B	C	D	E	F	G	H	I	J	K	L	M
26	25	24	23	22	21	20	19	18	17	16	15	14

N	O	P	Q	R	S	T	U	V	W	X	Y	Z
13	12	11	10	9	8	7	6	5	4	3	2	1

Quilt reads: THEY GO UNDERCOVER!

Task 47: Guilty Party

From page 94

Clara LeCheat committed the crime!

Evidence:

We know that exactly **four** lies were told . . .

- If it were Arnold, then three lies would have been told (by those who said it wasn't Arnold).
- If it were Bjorn, then two lies would have been told.
- If it were Clara, then **four** lies would have been told.
- If it were Davey, then three lies would have been told.
- If it were Eyeball, then three lies would have been told.
- If it were Fingers, then three lies would have been told.

In confirming Clara as the guilty party, we know that out of the eighteen statements, four were lies and fourteen statements were true.

Only Clara LeCheat was accused by exactly four people: Bjorn, Davey, Eyeball and Fingers, a lie in each case.

The suspects that told the truth were Arnold and (a rather careless) Clara.

Task 48: Where Next?

From page 96

BEAUTY SALON

Task 49: PIN Problem

From page 98

The 4-digit code is: 2 4 1 7

Task 50: Closing the Book

From page 100

The message reads: GOOD WORK, AGENT! YOU CRACKED THE CODE!